CAN YOU FIND IT?

25 LIBRARY SCAVENGER HUNTS TO SHARPEN YOUR RESEARCH SKILLS

Free Spirit
PUBLISHING

CAN YOU FIND IT?

25 LIBRARY SCAVENGER HUNTS TO SHARPEN YOUR RESEARCH SKILLS

RANDALL McCUTCHEON

Research Assistants:
Ellen Y. Brown, University of California at San Diego
Suzanne Carter, University of Michigan at Ann Arbor
Merry Hayes, University of Nebraska at Lincoln
Jane Raglin, University of Nebraska at Lincoln

Edited by Pamela Espeland

Library of Congress Cataloging-in-Publication Data
McCutcheon, Randall, 1949-
    Can you find it?: 25 library scavenger hunts to sharpen your research skills/Randall McCutcheon.
        p.   cm.
    Includes bibliographical references.
    ISBN 0-915793-14-8 (pbk.) :
    1. Libraries — Problems, exercises, etc. 2. Reference books
— Problems, exercises, etc. 3. Research — Methodology — Problems, exercises, etc. [1. Libraries — Problems, exercises, etc.
2. Reference books — Problems, exercises, etc.
3. Research — Methodology — Problems, exercises, etc.] I. Title.
Z710.M18 1989
028.7'076—dc19   88-19020
                                                          CIP
                                                           AC

Printed in the United States of America
10 9 8 7 6 5 4 3 2 1

Cover and text design: MacLean & Tuminelly

FREE SPIRIT PUBLISHING
123 N. Third St., Suite 716
Minneapolis, MN 55401
(612) 338-2068

Excerpt from HIGH SCHOOL on pages 17-18 by the Carnegie Foundation for the Advancement of Teaching. Copyright © 1983 by the Carnegie Foundation for the Advancement of Teaching. Reprinted by permission of Harper & Row.

"The Picnic" on pages 35-37 is copyright © 1955, 1960, 1961, 1962, 1963, 1964, 1965, 1966, 1967, 1968, 1969, 1970, 1973, 1981 by John Logan. "The Picnic" from *Only the Dreamer Can Change the Dream* by John Logan, first published by The Ecco Press in 1981. Reprinted by permission.

The John Simon review quoted on page 100 is copyright © 1975 by The New York Times Company. Reprinted by permission. (NOTE: Reference to John Simon review is found in Question 23.)

Excerpt from THE GREAT TELEVISION HEROES on pages 107-108 by Donald Glut and Jim Harmon. Copyright © 1975 by Donald Glut and Jim Harmon. Reprinted by permission of Doubleday, a division of Bantam, Doubleday, Dell Publishing Group, Inc.

The author and publisher gratefully acknowledge the following for granting us permission to use their words and pictures in *Can You Find It?*:

The Associated Press
Dave Barry
The Boston Globe
Ken Brown
The Christian Science Monitor
Chronicle Features
Contemporary Books, Inc.
Farrar, Straus and Giroux, Inc.
Seth Feinberg
FOLON/LE MONDE Paris
Games Magazine
Gorilla Graphics
Harper & Row, Publishers, Inc.
High School News
King Features Syndicate, Inc.
John Logan
Mark Twain Journal
Doug Marlette
Marvel Entertainment Group, Inc.
New Directions Publishing Corporation
NEWSWEEK
The New Yorker Magazine, Inc.
The Overlook Press and Stan Mack

George Price
PAJ Publications and Steve Tesich
PSC Games Limited Partnership
PUNCH
Random House, Inc.
David Rimmer
Peter Schickele
Bob Schochet
Paul Simon
Simon & Schuster, Inc.
Sports Illustrated
Martha Swope
Rosemary Thurber
Time Inc.
Tribune Media Services
UFS, Inc.
Universal Press Syndicate
Warner Books/New York
Warner/Chappell Music, Inc.
The Washington Post
Washington Post Writers Group
William Morris Agency, Inc.
World Press Review

For my grandmother

Acknowledgments

The Scavenger Hunts in *Can You Find It?* were created and developed over a four-year period. Hundreds of students successfully participated in the process. I especially want to thank the following people who gave me inspiration along the way.

Molly Ackerman

Roxana Alger

Ted Allen

Cecilia Andrews

Sarah Bynum

Robert Chen

Tricia Cheng

Dawn Clendenen

Barclay Feather

Emily Franklin

Amy Garwood

Susan Garwood

Austan Goolsbee

Nan Graf

Peg Hart

Barbara Hynes

Lynn Lu

Grace MacNamee

George Paul

Adam Rothman

James Schaffer

My former students at Milton Academy in Massachusetts, at Lincoln East High School in Nebraska, and at the Nebraska Scholars Institute

And to the staff at Cox Library, Milton Academy — thank you.

Contents

Foreword

We are in the midst, today, of a revolution, the transition from a manufacturing economy to one emphasizing services and information. Manufacturing industries are everywhere in decline. Industrialists of the future will build no railroads, invent few wonderful new means of fabrication. For the most part their business will be to assess what is known, to package information, and to pass it along to others for a price. Producers of new information will be vastly outnumbered by consumers. The workplaces of the future are the library and the computer console. How can our children be prepared for this brave new world?

They face no easy task. The libraries of Harvard University alone contain 11 million volumes. Assuming that each volume has about 150 pages, with about 400 words per page, we may calculate the store of wisdom at Harvard to run to approximately 660 billion words. If we assume that the accomplished reader can process about 50 words per minute, it is easy, for a skilled arithmetician at least, to estimate how long it would take to survey the material at Harvard. The answer is a staggering 25 thousand years, and that does not allow time for sleep or other distraction! Obviously we need a guide to the mine or mind field. Those who venture in blind are sure to get lost.

Randall McCutcheon has clearly recognized the problem. An introduction to the library should entail more than a tour of the premises. Yet that is about the limit of the help offered most of our students. Mr. McCutcheon has found a way to contribute and make it fun. His Scavenger Hunt is an inspired idea. Students are shown how to make their way through the maze. They learn how to focus their search, to separate the relevant from the irrelevant, to resist the temptation to explore intriguing sidetracks, to recognize the most direct path to the Holy Grail. Once they have found the way, they are eager and able to return.

1

Can You Find It? should be required reading for all. Library skills are as important as writing and arithmetic for those who venture into the information-service world. Education is the key. The information we need is in the library, but we must learn how to find it.

January 1989

Dr. Michael B. McElroy
Chairman of the Department
of Earth and Planetary Science
Harvard University

Introduction

If you are like most beginning researchers, you don't know how to play the game. Entering a library, you feel as if you are trapped inside some gigantic alien pinball machine — the ricochets random, the flippers frozen, the tilt inevitable. Thus, the time you spend "playing library" is largely wasted.

Why?

Because you assume that learning how to use library resources — learning how to master the game — *will be DULL, DULL, DULL.*

So you don't learn.

Maybe you've tried. Maybe you've actually picked up a book or two on How To Do Research In The Library. The trouble is, most of those books are just what you expect. Only more so.

Facts aren't always fun. (And that's a fact.)

This book is.

CALVIN and HOBBES by Bill Watterson

Unlike other books on How To Do Research In The Library, *Can You Find It?...*

- entertains you with irreverent humor (in quotes, quips, conundrums, and puns),

- treats you to some of the best writers and cartoonists from the past and of the present (from "Bloom County" to *Thurber & Company*, from Woody Allen to Whoopi Goldberg),

- gives you *hands-on* experience in the library (through dozens of intriguing Scavenger Hunts), and

- challenges you to become a Critical Thinker (each Scavenger Hunt forces you to *define* the real question, to *formulate* a research strategy, and to *use* the actual reference materials).

But *Can You Find It?* is more than an introduction to library research and to information literacy. It is, in its own way, a home-away-from-home entertainment center. Our purpose is to amuse as well as to bemuse. Too many people believe that libraries are merely repositories for snoring students, sedentary scholars, social misfits, and Soviet spies. True enough. However, a well-stocked library can also reveal answers to some of the world's most pertinent and pressing questions.

For example:

"How could you have a teacher arrested as a common nuisance?"

In teaching how to use the library effectively, we have posed this problem to hundreds of high-school and college students. Many have laughed. Others have offered the names of their least favorite teachers. All have agreed that we should ferret out these evildoers. But *not one* has been able to suggest a research strategy that might lead to a successful answer and subsequent arrest.

"Everybody is ignorant, only on
different subjects."

— *Will Rogers*

The process of finding the answer is significantly more important than finding the answer itself. Mastering that process — learning how to become a Critical Thinker — is what prepares you to find the answers that you will someday need. In fact, *once you have mastered that process, you can find out almost anything you want to know.* And that's what this book is *really* all about.

Information is power. Knowing how to locate that information gives you power.

Imagine, for a moment, that a certain teacher of your acquaintance actually deserves to be arrested as a public nuisance. The process of making that arrest happen involves identifying the key concepts in the research question (*how can one be arrested as a common nuisance?*) and then exploring some possible strategies. Your steps in Critical Thinking might include the following:

arrest...law...legal problem...need a legal definition of
"common nuisance"...need a specialized dictionary...
Black's Law Dictionary...find court cases cited...record
relevant criteria for being judged a "common
nuisance"...observe teacher behavior...
note similarities...phone police.

To help you develop your own Critical Thinking skills, *Can You Find It?* is divided into four parts.

• Part One: The Questions

The Scavenger Hunt format is structured to capture the imagination of even the most intransigent "deskperado." Each question is preceded by supporting material — cartoons, quotations, odd facts, humorous excerpts from various works of literature — chosen not only to enhance the meaning of the research problem but also to keep you intrigued. Look them over, then read the question. Or, if you prefer, jump ahead to the question before studying the supporting materials. Try to determine a research strategy based on what you learn from the question and the supporting materials. If this proves impossible, turn to the clues.

> "The way to do research is to to attack the
> facts at the point of greatest astonishment."
> — *Celia Green*

• Part Two: The Clues

The clues are written to suggest ways of Critically Thinking about the question. They point you toward specific places to begin your research. But they *don't* "spoonfeed" you. The impudent tone, the intentional ambiguity, and the ever-present wordplay make the clues a separate challenge in themselves. (Not all of them are helpful, for example. Some of them are just there. A lot like life.)

If, after studying the clues, you are *still* unable to determine a research strategy, you can turn to the answers. But don't give up *too* soon. Not getting there is half the fun.

• Part Three: The Answers

The answers not only tell you *where* you should have looked, they also tell you *why* you should have sought out that particular reference work.   And they describe other possible uses of that reference work (for future reference, naturally). So you should read them even if you do solve the Scavenger Hunts on your own.

Two important points to keep in mind:

• The answers to most of the questions can be found in more than one source.

• The answers sometimes vary in different editions of the same reference work, and when different reference works are checked against each other.

The references included in *Can You Find It?* were chosen, for the most part, because of their value as research tools. But our choice of sources should be just a beginning for you. If they stimulate your curiosity and make you want to go further and learn more (which we think they will), turn to the resources section.

• Part Four: Resources

The resources include suggestions for building your very own At-Home Reference Library and for adding to it as your thirst for knowledge continues to grow. (In our experience, nothing quenches that thirst quite as effectively as a big, fat book full of fascinating facts.) It also includes a list of the references cited in this book. That list is intended as an aid to teachers, librarians, and parents. If you read it BEFORE attempting to find the answers to the questions, then YOU ARE LAZY (not to mention cheating).

It is our hope that *Can You Find It?* will serve both as an introduction to some of the basic reference sources, and as a lasting lesson in Critical Thinking Skills.

So welcome to the wonderful and often wacky world of the Research Expert.

Randall McCutcheon
January 1989

Tips for Teachers, Librarians, and Parents

Can You Find It? is meant as a library guide for students lost in the "bewilderness" of thousands of possible research resources. It is meant to familiarize students with various ways to approach research, and with various places in the library they can go to find the answers to different types of questions. It is meant to increase their comfort level when confronted by countless card catalogs, seemingly endless shelves of reference works, and macro-files of microfilm.

The Scavenger Hunt approach gives you much flexibility in meeting the needs of individual students. For example:

- A student can embark on the Hunt as an independent self-help project. Or:

- An entire class can undertake the Hunt as a part of the normal curriculum.

We suggest using five class periods, with each period focusing on the following:

• Period 1: Preview and Assignments

Preview (first 20 minutes): Have the students read the Introduction, which explains how the book is organized. Discuss one or two of the questions with everyone. This discussion will acquaint the students with the process involved in finding the answers.

Assignments (second 20 minutes): Assign questions to the students (or let them choose the ones that interest them, after skimming the questions section).

Check the list of references on pages 192-194 against those available in the library in which your students will be working. This will enable you to pinpoint which questions the students should pursue. (The remaining questions, clues, and answers can be read and discussed in class at other times throughout the school year.)

SUGGESTION: We have found that students gain more from the Hunt if they are divided into research groups of three and are permitted to work together. Consider having the groups compete for prizes.

You may need to reserve library time. Consider going outside the school library and taking a field trip to a larger library in your area (such as a County Library or a local college or university library).

• Periods 2, 3, and 4: The Hunt

Start by making certain that students are aware of library etiquette. (See Question 16, "Moo-Goo-Gai-Panic," for suggestions.)

Before the students begin, explain that they may become frustrated but that they should not give up. If they spend more than 15 minutes on one question, they should move on to another and return to the original one later. (You don't want all the students working on the same question. You want them working on different ones so that they don't all follow the "smart kid" around.)

To make certain that students play fair, you might announce to them that you are temporarily removing one of the references from the library. This "missing" reference will force students to actually verify each answer and will deter them from simply turning to the back of the book. Furthermore, you should warn the students that different editions of a particular reference work will mean different page numbers for a given answer. You might require, therefore, that each student record the page numbers of found answers. These verification checks will encourage most students to dig in and get their hands dusty.

Supervise the Hunt closely so that you can spot the struggling students. Try giving them hints until they are able to find at least *one* correct answer. A little success will usually whet their appetite and instill in them the necessary confidence to go on.

DO NOT allow students to ask the librarian for help. The whole point of the Hunt is to teach them to think for themselves.

• Period 5: Debriefing

Review with the students what they should have learned, and explain how they can apply that knowledge in other ways. (You may want to discuss with them other relevant reference works that are not included in the answers.)

Allow time for students to describe interesting or unusual experiences they may have had during the Hunt, and to explain in their own words the kinds of things they learned along the way.

"Obviously, research is not an end in itself. The day comes when the pleasures and drudgery of the detective hunt are over and the report must be written."

— Jacques Barzun and Henry F. Graff,
The Modern Researcher

If you choose to use *Can You Find It?* throughout the school year to support specific research projects or simply to enhance your students' research skills, you may condense this five-period process in whatever way suits your needs.

Finally: We have made every effort to make *Can You Find It?* as accurate and helpful as possible. If you discover what you believe are *better* answers to any of the questions than the ones we've provided, please send them to:

Randall McCutcheon
c/o Free Spirit Publishing
123 North Third Street, Suite 716
Minneapolis, MN 55401

We're also very interested in hearing about your experiences in using this book. Please write to us! And we'd be delighted to receive any suggestions for questions for future editions.

We welcome your comments.

Key to Symbols
Used in *Can You Find It?*

The following symbols, developed especially for *Can You Find It?* and used throughout this book, serve at least two purposes: They function as graphic clues, and they tell you something about what you are going to see or read.

 Quote from Book

 Song Lyrics

 Quote from Magazine

 The Question

 Quote from Newspaper

 Clues

 Quote from Play

 The Answer

PART ONE

The Questions

1

Assessing the SAT

ARE YOU A GENIUS OR AN IDIOT?

The capital of Malawi is _____?

       (A) Washington, D.C.
       (B) Paris
       (C) Tokyo
       (D) London
       (E) Zomba

Adam Robinson and John Katzman, *The Princeton Review: Cracking the System: The SAT* (New York: Villard Books, 1986), pp. 7 and 12.

HIGH SCHOOL NEWS

The Scholastic Aptitude Test (SAT) is:

- A clever device used by the educational establishment to avoid its responsibilities.

- A hurdle of much-exaggerated importance for high school seniors trying to get into college.

- One symbol of what's wrong with the high school education system in America.

The SAT itself does not allow an answer of "all of the above," but in this case, that is the correct answer. The declining status and significance of this test is one sign that the hidebound American secondary educational system is at last undergoing some significant changes.

Old institutions die slowly, and the SAT still has a powerful mystique. It remains a tense rite of passage for nearly half of all high school seniors. Yesterday, some 267,000 filed nervously into classrooms and auditoriums around the country to agonize over its multiple choice questions about vocabulary, grammar and math.

Dan Morgan, "SAT's are getting in the way of education,"
The Washington Post, January 29, 1984. Used with permission
of *The Washington Post*.

The SAT was developed at a time when many believed an instrument could be prepared to measure "aptitude" — a relatively constant set of intellectual characteristics and abilities not seriously affected by previous education. Now substantial evidence suggests that this early faith was misplaced. Today it is generally acknowl-edged that the SAT does not measure aptitude, nor is it directly linked to the curriculum in the schools. Still, the nation has mistakenly come to view the SAT as a reliable report card on the nation's schools.

The SAT also was created at a time when the quality of high schools was extremely uneven, and when ethnic and racial intolerance was a harsh reality in the admissions procedure. The SAT sought to make the process of student selection more accurate and equitable. And SAT scores were given considerable weight in selecting students. Today, the majority of higher learning institutions are not highly selective, and there are few that use the SAT as the primary criterion for choosing students.

Moreover, the SAT is not very helpful in predicting how a student is likely to do in college. When used alone, the SAT is somewhat better than random selection in predicting academic success. When the SAT score and high school grades are combined, the accuracy of predicting success in college modestly increases. Still, we are concerned about the inflated attention given the SAT at a time when colleges are less inclined to screen students out. We are also concerned that this major testing effort is limited to the college bound. We conclude, therefore, that while the SAT has performed a successful purpose in the past, it will have a decreasingly important role to play in years ahead.

Ernest L. Boyer, "The Carnegie Foundation Report on Secondary Education in America," 1987. Reprinted by permission of Harper & Row.

"An incompetent teacher is even worse than an incompetent surgeon because a surgeon can only cut up one person at a time."

— *Ernest Boyer*

EXAMPLE:
BRAINS:TEST WRITER

(A) lips:chicken   (B) clock:moron
(C) cap:dunce   (D) meat:head
(E) dumb:bunny

Choice (A) is the correct answer.

Henry Beard, *The No Sweat Aptitude Test (NSAT)* (New York: Harper & Row, Publishers, 1988), p. 13.

"The Carnegie Foundation Report on Secondary Education in America" recommends a new assessment test to replace the SAT. What would this new test be called?

Need more clues? See pages 113-115.

2
Ask Not...

COINCIDENCE OR NOT?

- Both the names "Kennedy" and "Lincoln" have 7 letters.
- Both presidents were assassinated by men with 15 letters in their names: Lee Harvey Oswald and John Wilkes Booth.
- Lincoln was shot in a theater and his assassin ran to a warehouse. Kennedy was shot from a warehouse and his assassin ran to a theater.
- Lincoln's secretary was named Kennedy. Kennedy's secretary was named Lincoln.
- Both men were succeeded in office by men named "Johnson"; the names "Andrew Johnson" and "Lyndon Johnson" both have 13 letters.
- Lincoln was a Republican; Kennedy was a Demmocratt. Both parties have 10 letters in their names.
- Both men left widows who eventually married Greek shipping magnates; both men had children named Tod.
- Mrs. Kennedy liked bananas; Mrs. Lincoln went bananas.

- Both men feared nuclear war with the Soviet Union.

- Kennedy's middle name was "Gettysburg"; Lincoln's middle name was "Bay of Pigs."

- Kennedy was a Catholic; Lincoln was a Satanist. Both religions have 8 letters in their names.

- Both men had affairs with Marilyn Monroe; both men were played by William Devane in television movies.

- Lincoln fought a war against "The South"; Kennedy fought a war against "Vietnam." Both countries have sneaky, devious citizens.

- Both men were "President" at the time they were shot; the word "President" has 9 letters.

Dan Carlinsky, ed., *College Humor* (New York: Harper & Row, 1982), p. 193.

ROBOTMAN

President John F. Kennedy, on the night of April 29, 1962, gave a White House dinner to honor Nobel Prize Winners. Present were Nobel laureates and 124 other scientists, writers, editors, and educators. On the front page of the *New York Times*, the President was quoted as describing the dinner as "probably the greatest concentration of talent and genius in this house..." since when?

Need more clues? See page 116.

3
Nerds and Knotheads

...the term [nerd] apparently derives from hot-rodder and surfer jargon of the mid-1960s. (We nerds do our research.) It referred then to an inept, ineffectual person — any jerk who wasn't into carburetors or waves, presumably — but by the time the word entered general usage it had acquired the additional connotation of high intelligence. A nerd was known, 20 years ago, as a "brain." Thirty years ago, a nerd was an "egghead," like Adlai Stevenson. None of these terms, please note, was bestowed with any affection whatever.

Paula Span, *The Boston Globe Magazine*, February 1, 1987, p. 20. Reprinted courtesy of The Boston Globe.

"...yet how is it these vital facts are virtually unknown in this country today?"

If in addition to being physically unattractive you find that you do not get along well with others, do not under any circumstances attempt to alleviate this situation by developing an interesting personality. An interesting personality is, in an adult, insufferable. In a teenager it is frequently punishable by law.

Fran Lebowitz, *Social Studies* (New York: Random House, 1981), p. 25.

The slang expression "knothead" was first used in what popular work of American literature?

Need more clues? See pages 117-118.

4
Mall-Adjusted

"The'80s have added yet another fear to
the growing list of shoppers
everywhere...Mallphobia, the terror of not
being able to find your car after you have
shopped in the mall."

— *Erma Bombeck*

What a great place for a shopping mall

Scalera postcard; © 1987 Gorilla Graphics.

In describing the world's largest shopping mall, William Severini Kowinski wrote, "[It] contains the world's largest indoor amusement park and the largest indoor water park. It has the planet's biggest parking lot. According to Nader Ghermezian, one of the four brothers who devised and built it, it is the most complete tourist attraction in the Universe." Name the mall.

Need more clues? See page 119-120.

5
Back in the U.S.S.R.

Remember the old stereotype of the Soviet woman? There she strides, all 180 pounds of her, factory pants flapping in the wind, red banners flying all about her, her throaty voice uplifted in praise of Marx and tractors. And today's young woman? You have a right to expect change but — the Watusi? Sleeping car sex? Fashionable vacations on the Black Sea?...as revolutions go, things have surely changed.

Guido Gerosa, "Sex on the Leningrad Night Train," *Atlas World Press Review*, November 1969, p. 39.

"I'm very interested in sex education. What would you recommend?"

Drawing by Ross; ©1973 The New Yorker Magazine, Inc.

Although many Soviet educators were opposed, mandatory sex education classes have begun in the Soviet Union. The classes are being offered as a response to sexual problems linked to the nation's soaring divorce rate. However, on January 13, 1985, Tass, the Soviet News Agency, reported on the compulsory classes without mentioning the word "sex." According to Tass, the classes consist of what?

Need more clues? See pages 121-122.

6
It Must Be Love

"I'd trade a year in heaven for a day with you my dear."

Dave Van Ronk, from the song "Another Time and Place."

"Moons and Junes and ferris wheels,
The dizzy, dancing way you feel,
As every fairy tale comes real,
I've looked at love that way."

"And when you ran to me
your cheeks flushed with the night
we walked on frosted fields
of juniper and lamplight
I held your hand...."

"Hearts will never be practical until they can
be made unbreakable."
— *The Wizard of Oz*

It is the picnic with Ruth in the spring.
Ruth was third on my list of seven girls
But the first two were gone (Betty) or else
Had someone (Ellen has accepted Doug).
Indian Gully the last day of school;
Girls make the lunches for the boys too.
I wrote a note to Ruth in algebra class
Day before the test. She smiled, and nodded.
We left the cars and walked through the young corn
The shoots green as paint and the leaves like tongues
Trembling. Beyond the fence where we stood
Some wild strawberry flowered by an elm tree
And Jack-in-the-pulpit was olive ripe.
A blackbird fled as I crossed, and showed
A spot of gold or red under its quick wing.
I held the wire for Ruth and watched the whip
Of her long, striped skirt as she followed.
Three freckles blossomed on her thin, white back
Underneath the loop where the blouse buttoned.
We went for our lunch away from the rest,
Stretched in the new grass, our heads close
Over unknown things wrapped up in wax papers.
Ruth tried for the same, I forget what it was,
And our hands were together. She laughed,
And a breeze caught the edge of her little
Collar and the edge of her brown, loose hair
That touched my cheek. I turned my face in-
To the gentle fall. I saw how sweet it smelled.
She didn't move her head or take her hand.

I felt a soft caving in my stomach
As at the top of the highest slide
When I had been a child, but was not afraid,
And did not know why my eyes moved with wet
As I brushed her cheek with my lips and brushed
Her lips with my own lips. She said to me
Jack, Jack, different than I had ever heard,
Because she wasn't calling me, I think,
Or telling me. She used my name to
Talk in another way I wanted to know.
She laughed again and then she took her hand;
I gave her what we had both touched — can't
Remember what it was, and we ate the lunch.
Afterward we walked in the small, cool creek
Our shoes off, her skirt hitched, and she smiling,
My pants rolled, and then we climbed up the high
Side of Indian Gully and looked
Where we had been, our hands together again.
It was then some bright thing came in my eyes,
Starting at the back of them and flowing
Suddenly through my head and down my arms
And stomach and my bare legs that seemed not
To stop in feet, not to feel the red earth
Of the Gully, as though we hung in a
Touch of birds. There was a word in my throat
With the feeling and I knew the first time
What it meant and I said, it's beautiful.
Yes, she said, and I felt the sound and word
In my hand join the sound and word in hers
As in one name said, or in one cupped hand.
We put back on our shoes and socks and we
Sat in the grass awhile, crosslegged, under
A blowing tree, not saying anything.
And Ruth played with shells she found in the creek,

As I watched. Her small wrist which was so sweet
To me turned by her breast and the shells dropped
Green, white, blue, easily into her lap,
Passing light through themselves. She gave the pale
Shells to me, and got up and touched her hips
With her light hands, and we walked down slowly
To play the school games with the others.

Name the title and author of this poem.

Need more clues? See pages 123-124.

7
Bach-Analia

Dear Mr. Kelly,

I'm truly sorry my extra credit essay, "The Beatles: The Message in the Music" contained eight run-on sentences, six sentence fragments, excessive use of commas, countless subject/verb disagreements, and improper use of the semicolon...Putrid...As for your comment that the Beatles' songs are not a suitable subject for composition, may I refer you to Leonard Bernstein's statement in the current issue of *Time* magazine that "The Beatles' melodies are equal to those of Franz Schubert," and to Kenneth Tynan's in the same issue that "The Beatles' lyrics are often reminiscent of T.S. Eliot." And I'm very sorry, no, *distressed,* to learn that in *your* day you weren't allowed to write English essays on the Music of Glenn Miller...Whoever *he* was....

Yours sincerely,
Patricia Dugan
English 12-B
3rd Period

P.S. May I also remind you that while your subjects and your verbs agree, what you practice and what you preach *don't*...You two-faced....

David Rimmer, *Album* (New York: Dramatists Play Services, Inc., 1981), p. 42.
Reprinted by permission of the playwright. (Also published by Nelson Doubleday, Inc., Garden City, New York.)

"I only know two pieces — one is 'Clair de Lune' and the other one isn't."

— Victor Borge

"*This song describes the events of a lovely spring day. The sky is a cloudless blue, birds are singing, and out at the ballpark the grass is an emerald green. It's the top of the fourth, there are two out and runners on first and second. The batter hits a slow roller down the third-base line. The third baseman scoops up the ball barehanded and tries for a force play at second . . .*"

In the spring of 1953 the author completed his high school 4H club dissertation on Johann Sebastian Bach's relationship to food, with special emphasis on the *Coffee Cantata,* one of Johann Sebastian's rare ventures into the field of gastronomy. That summer saw the author in Europe searching for the manuscripts of other J.S. Bach cantatas, many of which have never been found, and his poor financial condition forced the author on many occasions to sing for his supper, which, his singing being what it was, usually consisted of stale bread and water. Upon biting into one particularly stiff slice of bread, however, he perceived that what he had first taken to be spots of black mold were actually musical notes written in a rather tasty ink and that the bread was not bread at all but was, in reality, a portion of a pile of manuscript pages that had become stuck together and browned with age. Tracing the origin of this serendipitous supper led the author to the ancient Leckendachschloss,[3] in southern Bavaria, where he found the complete manuscript of a *Sanka Cantata,* "by P.D.Q. Bach composed," being employed as a strainer in the caretaker's percolator. A cursory perusal of the music immediately revealed the reason for the atrocious taste of the coffee, but the author's curiosity was piqued by the juxtaposition of such a famous family name and such completely unfamiliar initials, so he purchased the limp and dripping manuscript for a few *Pfennigs* and took it back to the University of Southern North Dakota at Hoople, where he had been engaged to teach in the fall.

---

[3] "The Castle of the Leaking Roof." In the eighteenth century its flat roof was covered to a depth of about a foot with finely ground coffee beans; these dried in the sun until the next rainstorm, at which time pots and pans were placed on the floor under the leaks in the roof, and the world's largest coffee-maker was set into operation, providing (after a typical forty-five-minute downpour) enough coffee to keep the entire town of Klatsch awake for a month.

In what year did Johann Sebastian Bach compose the *Coffee Cantata*?

Need more clues? See pages 125-126.

8
Ducks in the Wry

Suddenly, Professor Liebowitz realizes he has come to the seminar without his duck.

I recently learned of a group called The Society of Future Ducks, which is for people who would like to be reincarnated as ducks. Readers may contact them at Department BW, P.O. Box 1497, Easton, PA 18042.

Bill S. Evans
Bedford, MA

"You know those ducks in that lagoon right near Central Park South? That little lake? By any chance, do you know where they go, the ducks, when it gets all frozen over? Do you happen to know, by any chance?"

— *Holden Caulfield*

SALINGER'S HOLDEN CAULFIELD
Among the young, the mad, the saintly.

Russell Hoban, *Time,* September 15, 1961, p. 84.

In the first place, it was a dumb question. "Who are the ten most admired men in America today and why." That's almost as dumb as when they ask you what you want to be when you grow up. And so I wrote your name ten times. Holden Caulfield. Holden Caulfield. Holden Caulfield. Holden Caulfield. Holden Caulfield. Holden Caulfield. Holden Caulfield. Holden Caulfield. Holden Caulfield. Holden Caulfield. "Because he's not a phony" and I got an

"F." And then my parents had to talk to Mr. Bartlett, our principal, and they all decided they didn't know what to do with me and then I had to go see Mr. Bartlett with them and they told me there was no way anyone anywhere could answer Holden Caulfield as even one of the ten most admired men in America today on his civics test and get away with it and how Miss Pearce had practically had a hemorrhage when she read my paper because she had such high hopes for me this semester and I would have to apologize to her and who the hell was Holden Caulfield anyway?

"Where has Tommy Flowers Gone?" All rights reserved. Copyright, 1972, by Terrence McNally.

Copies of *Catcher in the Rye* that have been checked out in public libraries in Chicago and never returned: 7,500.

Lewis H. Lapham, Michael Pollan, and Eric Etheridge, *The Harpers Index Book* (New York: Henry Holt and Company, 1987), p. 23.

The *San Francisco Chronicle's* review of *The Catcher in the Rye* concluded that "Mr. Salinger's novel is funny, poignant, and is in its implications, profound. It is literature of a very high order. It really is." Who wrote this review?

Need more clues? See page 127.

9
A Goldberg Variation

© 1984 Martha Swope. Reprinted with permission.

Mike Nichols once described actress/comedienne Whoopi Goldberg as "one part Elaine May, one part Groucho, one part Ruth Draper, one part Richard Pryor, and five parts never seen before."

Whoopi Goldberg was born in 1950 in New York City. Her first stage experience came at the age of eight at the Helena Rubinstein Children's Theatre. However, it was a long and arduous road to the resounding success of her one-woman Broadway show during the 1984-1985 theatrical season. In fact, at one point after graduating from beauty college, Whoopi took a job at a mortuary, dressing the hair of and applying the makeup to corpses.

Whoopi later revealed that her mortuary job was "great work" because she was "tired of working on living people who all wanted to" what?

Need more clues? See page 128.

10
Much Ado About Everything

*"You're going to quote me out of context
just once too often."*

LESSON 6: QUOTING OTHER AUTHORS

If placed in a situation where you must quote another author, always write "[sic]" after any word that may be misspelled or looks the least bit questionable in any way. If there are no misspellings or curious words, toss in a few "[sic]"s just to break up the flow. By doing this, you will appear to be knowledgeable and "on your toes," while the one quoted will seem suspect and vaguely discredited. Two examples will suffice:

> *"O Sleepless as the river under thee,*
> *Vaulting the sea, the prairies' dreaming sod,*
> *Unto us lowliest sometime sweep, descend*
> *And of the curveship [sic] lend a myth to God."*
> *—Hart Crane*

> *"Beauty is but a flowre [sic],*
> *Which wrinckles [sic] will devoure [sic],*
> *Brightnesse [sic] falls from the ayre [sic],*
> *Queenes [sic] have died yong [sic] and faire [sic],*
> *Dust hath closde [sic] Helens [sic] eye [sic].*
> *I am sick [sic], I must dye [sic]:*
> * Lord, have mercy on us."*
> *—Thomas Nashe*

Note how only one small "[sic]" makes Crane's entire stanza seem trivial and worthless, which, in his case, takes less doing than most. Nashe, on the other hand, has been rendered virtually unreadable. Anyone having to choose between you and Nashe would pick you every time! And, when it's all said and done, isn't that the name of the game?

Michael O'Donoghue, *How to Write Good* (New York: Simon & Schuster, Inc., 1987), p. 42.

SHOE   by Jeff MacNelly

"The surest way to make a monkey out of a
man is to quote him."

— *Robert Benchley*

"Knowing I lov'd my books, he furnish'd me,
From mine own library with volumes that
I prize above my dukedom."
This quotation is taken from what famous play?

Need more clues? See pages 129-130.

11
Rated R

> "If you kept seeing Robert Redford stark naked on the screen, would he be a superstar today? No way. Or Gene Hackman showing everything? Their million dollar days would be over. I want to be in a movie where all the men take their clothes off and I don't."
>
> — *Cybill Shepherd*

Customs do change. Babylonian law decreed drowning as the proper punishment for a woman accused of adultery. But if she floated after being forced to jump into a sacred river, she was judged innocent. In the Middle Ages, someone who had sexual relations with a Jew could be punished by burial alive; adulterers were flogged through the streets; prostitutes had their noses slit; and men were burned alive for having sex with dogs, goats, cows, even geese.

In the Enlightenment of the 18th century, the Austrian Empress Maria Theresa appointed a troop of spies known as Commissioners

of Chastity to enforce her prim views. Said the irrepressible
Giacomo Casanova: "They carried off to prison, at all hours of the
day and from all the streets of Vienna, poor girls whom they found
alone, who in most cases went out only to earn an honest living."
Sodomy was long considered a capital offense, and the Marquis de
Sade was sentenced to death for engaging in it. Hitler threw
homosexuals into concentration camps. In recent years the
resurgence of Islamic law means that adulterers face flogging in
countries like Iran, Saudi Arabia, Pakistan. And down through the
centuries, despite all the decrees, people have gone right on, of
course, enjoying sex as best they could.

"AT LAST, A MOVIE WITHOUT ALL THOSE FILTHY SEX SCENES!"

The "first motion picture sex shocker" premiered on October 17, 1916 at the Lyric Theatre in New York City. The movie starred Annette Kellerman, who, according to a reviewer of the time, "wanders disconsolately...through the film, all undressed and nowhere to go." What was the title of this film?

Need more clues? See pages 131-132.

12
A Conscientious Objection

"It's hard to believe that everything <u>doesn't</u> have a military solution."

In 1917, the first woman ever to be elected to Congress voted against our participation in World War I. (She was joined by forty-nine other members of Congress.) Ernestine Evans, who was in the balcony at the time, said, "She did not merely vote 'No' but in a voice low and fraught with emotion, half rising from her seat, she said: 'I want to stand by my country but I cannot vote for war.'" (Reported in *Scribner's Commentator*, November 1941, p. 27.)

On December 8, 1941, an outspoken and courageous woman voiced the single "Nay" vote against the joint resolution that would declare a state of war between the United States and the Imperial Government of Japan. What was her name?

Need more clues? See pages 133-134.

13
Oliver Twisted

I was told I was adopted when I was about two, but I had no idea what it meant. When my parents said, "You're adopted," I thought they were saying, "You're a doctor," and I kept telling them, "No, I am not a doctor!" I hated the idea of being a doctor because I hated doctors. I still hate them because I can't stand shots.

Timmy, age 12, in *How It Feels to be Adopted* by Jill Krementz (New York: Alfred A. Knopf, 1982), p. 19.

I don't know how old I was when they put me in the orphanage...not very...and the first time I heard the word "orphan" I thought it was this guy's name. Billy Orphan. Then I found out that I was an orphan too. And I figured that Billy and I were related. But then I found out that we were all orphans...and I figured... hell...somebody must be lying...we can't all be relatives.

So we were all orphans but I still didn't know what the word meant except that we talked about everything in terms of that one word...the outside world was a non-orphanage...those that got placed were de-orphanated...those that came back were re-orphanated. For a long time I thought only boys were orphans...so when I grew up I wanted to be a girl. Then I found out that there were female orphans too...we called them orphenes. But I still didn't know what the word meant. So I asked one of the guards one day...what's an orphan? He said it was somebody that nobody liked.

But these other orphans liked me...Billy liked me...so I asked him if that made me a non-orphan. He said no...he said being liked by another orphan didn't count.

In 1982, how many American children under age 18 had been "full" orphans at any time? ("Full" orphans are those who have lost both parents.)

Need more clues? See pages 135-136.

14
Gobble Gobble Glup Glup

A thousand hairy savages
Sitting down for lunch
Gobble gobble glup glup
Munch munch munch.

Spike Milligan, *Silly Verses for Kids;* quoted in J.M. and M.J. Cohen, *The Penguin Dictionary of Modern Quotations,* second edition (New York: Penguin Books, 1980), p. 234.

"MTV's amuck in America."
— *Martha Quinn,* MTV veejay

In Galesburg, Illinois, three college professors calling themselves terrorists of the Cultural Liberation Organization "executed" three freshmen before a mock firing squad because of intellectual apathy.

CLO leaders said the attack at Knox College was triggered by frustration with students who are uninterested in their classes and the world around them.

Authorities said the three faculty members, disguised in paramilitary garb and carrying realistic-looking weapons, burst into an unsuspecting class of freshman students, overturning tables and shouting obscenities.

The "terrorists" lined the entire class up against a wall with their hands and feet spread and picked out three students who had been particularly apathetic and nonparticipatory.

The students were tried by their classmates on charges of "intellectual apathy" and "crimes against Knox College" before receiving a punishment of death by firing squad.

The convicted students were roped together with their hands behind their backs and placed before a brick wall. After the prisoners were blindfolded, the chief terrorist "executed" them with a blank-filled .38-caliber starter's gun.

The professors said the class had one of its best discussions at its next meeting.

Art Peterson, *Teachers: A Survival Guide for the Grown-Up in the Classroom* (New York: Plume/New American Library, 1985), pp. 76-77.

MR. MUFFLER RUNS AMOK

And in the M&M Disco and Bait Shop, a hairy, leathery little backwoods hippie, who called himself Pisswilliger and looked like a three-day-old road-kill, told us he'd just finished pulling two years in the state pen. Too polite to ask what he'd been in for, we inquired instead what he intended to do, now that he was out. *"Do?"* he cried indignantly. "I ain't gonna do nothing, by God! They wouldn't let me do what I wanna do, so I ain't gonna do nothing, by God!" Well, we asked, what was it you *wanted* to do, Pisswilliger? "Why," he fumed, "I wanted to sell pot and pills to the high school kids, by God!"

Like the onset of puberty, running amok is just a "phrase" we all go through. What is the origin of the expression, "run amok"?

Need more clues? See pages 137-138.

15
Days of Our Lives

"Well, what'll we do today?"

Take off your shoes, put up your feet, sit back and relax. There's no other appropriate way to spend National Nothing Day. The un-holiday, noted by its fans yesterday, was the brainchild of newspaperman Harold Pullman Coffin, who thought Americans needed a day without celebrating, observing, or honoring anything. Since Coffin dreamed up the idea in 1973, people have been doing nothing about it ever since. For instance, take University of South Florida president John Lott Brown, who wouldn't say if or how he would observe the day. "I have nothing to say about nothing," he said. For those who can't bear to stand idle, even for one day, there was another option: Yesterday was also National Hat Day, in tribute to that once ever-so-necessary accessory.

The Boston Globe, January 17, 1987, p. 2. Reprinted courtesy of The Boston Globe.

Known as the "Mardi Gras of the North," the Anchorage Fur Rendezvous is a 10-day, community-wide celebration. Highlights of the festival include the annual World Championship Sled Dog Races, a Miners and Trappers Ball, and the famous Eskimo Blanket Toss. In what month is the Anchorage Fur Rendezvous celebrated?

Need more clues? See page 139.

16
Moo-Goo-Gai-Panic

PEKING (AP) — Do observe public order, respect the aged and be polite. Don't gamble, spit, or kill beneficial insects. Those are some of the recommendations to the citizens of Tianjin published by a Chinese newspaper Thursday, in a list of "Dos and don'ts" that kept alive a "time-honored custom of codifying, then numbering, proper behavior."

The official *Guangming Daily*, China's intellectual paper, published the Tianjin list Thursday. The residents of the country's fourth-largest city were told:

— Do abide by discipline and the law, love work, observe public order, cherish the aged and teachers and love the young, be polite, help and love each other, defend national honor and self-respect, protect public property, pay attention to hygiene and beautify the environment.

— Don't spit, litter, scrawl graffiti or put up posters everywhere, erect unauthorized sheds, pick flowers or break twigs off trees, block traffic, swear, make scenes in public, catch or kill beneficial insects and birds or gamble or indulge in superstition.

Lincoln Star, March 22, 1985, p. 26. Reprinted with permission of The Associated Press.

"Nothing happens next. This is it."

Drawing by Gahan Wilson; © 1980 The New Yorker Magazine, Inc.

Chinese "ratatouille" — In some rural areas of China it was reported that the popularity of rat steaks and rat-skin shoes has helped to control the pests that are said to consume 15 million tons of grain a year. It was reported that in areas of southern China, live rats were sold for 50 cents a pound, about the same as chicken. In Fujian Province, people hail rat steaks as the best steak in the world.

1986 World Almanac & Book of Facts, p. 716.

Q. Do people anywhere in the world eat out in restaurants more frequently than Americans?
A. Restaurant authorities believe the Chinese lead the world in restaurant dining. At least half of the people in Canton eat breakfast outside their homes; Shanghai has 12,000 restaurants; in Peking, 24-hour restaurants are commonplace. China's earliest restaurants, incidentally, were established during the T'ang Dynasty.

Omaha World Herald, January 4, 1987, p. 4 of the special section, *Sunday World Herald Magazine of the Midlands.*

A 26-year-old long-distance operator dubbed "China's walking telephone book" has memorized 15,000 phone numbers in 10 cities but hopes to do better, the Xinhua News Agency said. Gou Yanling, an operator in the northeastern city of Harbin, demonstrated her memory Saturday before 1,000 people attending a five-day telecommunications meeting in the capital. In response to queries from the audience, Gou "quickly and correctly" recited telephone numbers from several cities, including Peking, Dalian, Harbin, Shanghai and Tianjin, Xinhua said. Xinhua, which called her "China's walking telephone book," said she started work as an operator in 1981 and has perfected six methods of memorizing phone numbers "in order to improve service." She said she knows

15,000 telephone numbers in 10 cities. "I often memorize telephone numbers when I watch television, see advertisements, or pass shops and factories," Gou told Xinhua. "I will continue my efforts to improve service and will try to memorize 18,000 telephone numbers by August next year."

Boston Globe, November 24, 1986, p. 2. Reprinted courtesy of The Boston Globe.

You have decided to vacation in China next year. Planning ahead, you choose to call overseas and make dinner reservations at a restaurant in Peking. Unfortunately, you don't know the names or phone numbers of any restaurants in Peking. Where might you turn for help?

Need more clues? See pages 140-142.

17
One Small Stumble

"What we will have attained when Neil
Armstrong steps down upon the moon is a
completely new step in the evolution of man."

— Wernher Von Braun

"Beautiful, beautiful, beautiful.
A magnificent desolation."

— "Buzz" Aldrin, the second man to set foot on the moon

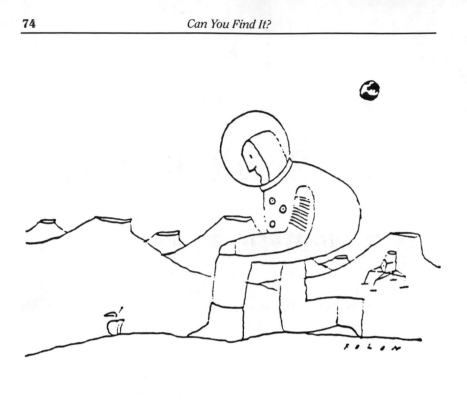

FOLON/MONDE Paris (July 1969). Used with permission.

"I leave you with the good advice my
father gave me when I left my home planet
of Vulcan — 'don't let the earth get
in your eyes.'"

— Mr. Spock

"Son, your mother is a remarkable woman."

Drawing by S. Gross; © 1983 The New Yorker Magazine, Inc.

"The ghostly, white-clad figure slowly descended the ladder. Having reached the bottom rung, he lowered himself into the bowl-shaped footpad of Eagle, the spindly lunar module of Apollo 11. Then he extended his left foot, cautiously, tentatively, as if testing water in a pool — and, in fact, testing a wholly new environment for man. That groping foot, encased in a heavy multilayered boot (size 9 1/2 B), would remain indelible in the minds of millions who watched it on TV, and a symbol of man's determination to step — and forever keep stepping — toward the unknown.

"After a few short but interminable seconds, U.S. Astronaut Neil Armstrong placed his foot firmly on the fine-grained surface of the moon. The time was 10:56 p.m. (E.D.T.), July 20, 1969. Pausing briefly, the first man on the moon spoke the first words on lunar soil...."

Time, July 25, 1969, p. 10. Reprinted by permission from *Time.*

The words were reported differently in *Time* magazine and the *Encyclopaedia Britannica* (fifteenth edition). What was that difference?

Need more clues? See page 143.

18
You Can Bet on It

THIS SPUD'S FOR YOU

Legendary athletes are honored when their number is retired
with them. Just ask Dave ("Spuds") Bresnahan, the never-to-be-
forgotten second-string catcher for the Williamsport (Pa.) Bills, a
class AA team. His immortal feat on the diamond last year
prompted 2,700 of his fans to gather at Bowman Field last week to
pay him a belated tribute and to paint his number, 59, on the
outfield fence.

With his hapless team 27 games out of first place and losing as
usual, Bresnahan had fired an errant pick-off throw over the third
baseman's head. As the runner came home, Dave triumphantly

tagged him out; he had held onto the ball while tossing an Idaho potato carved to look like a baseball. Unamused, the umpire ruled that the run had scored. Dave's angry manager got him kicked off the team. Last week Bresnahan, now a real estate salesman, was vindicated. "Gehrig had to hit .340 and play in more than 2,000 games to get his number retired," he boasted. "All I had to do is hit less than .150 and throw a potato."

Time "American Notes," June 13, 1988, p. 33. Reprinted by permission from *Time*.

"Now if Johnny has 87 cents and find 14 cents, then mugs a drunk for 56 cents, and bets it at 3 to 1 on a horse..."

Phi Delta Kappan, February 1986, p. 451. Reprinted from *Phi Delta Kappan* with permission of Bob Schochet.

"I used to be a gambler. But now I just make mental bets. That's how I lost my mind."

— Steve Allen

On Super Sunday, when more money is bet than on any other day, let's talk about odds.

What are the odds, in this nation of 240 million, that, in any given year, someone you know will play in the Super Bowl? If you assume, for argument's sake, that each of the 80 players in today's game will know 240 people individually, the chances that a random American will know a player are about one in 12,500.

What are the odds that you will know someone who'll contract AIDS? Between 1.5 and 3 million Americans already carry the virus, says a doctor at Walter Reed Army Medical Center. At the lower figure, the odds of you already knowing someone carrying the virus are one in 160. At the higher figure, the odds are one in 80. Split the difference, and on average, one American in 120 is carrying the acquired immune deficiency syndrome virus.

If, for argument's sake, each of us knows 240 people on an individual basis, then two people you know are already carrying the AIDS virus. It is roughly 100 times more likely that you'll know someone carrying the AIDS virus than that you'll be on speaking terms with a Denver Bronco or a New York Giant.

David Nyhan, *The Boston Globe,* January 25, 1987, p. A29. Reprinted courtesy of The Boston Globe.

In 1982, Ernie Kaufman gave tips on "baseball betting" in *Barron's*. Among his illegal and risky suggestions was the following:

"Another thing to consider is the knuckleball effect. In 1978, Pete Rose, then with the Cincinnati Reds...had a 44-game hitting streak — the longest in National League history. There was an enormous amount of pressure on Rose every day, but he said he felt it especially in any game played a day after he faced a knuckleball pitcher. Knucklers, he complained, ruin a hitter's timing: 'It's the next game in which you pay the penalty, because your timing is off.' Such an observation, coming from possibly the best hitter in baseball, supports the conclusion that a friendly wagerer should bet against any team that plays a game immediately after facing a knuckleball thrower, such as Charlie Hough of the Texas Rangers, Joe Niekro of the Houston Astros, his brother Phil, of the Atlanta Braves, or Burt Hooten of the Dodgers (possessor of the 'knuckle curve')."

According to Mr. Kaufman, how often does this strategy pay off?

Need more clues? See pages 144-145.

19

Gogh for It

The first art was created by primitive people, who made pots and plates with primitive decorations. They didn't realize this was art. They thought it was just pots and plates. Their problem was that seconds after they made a pot or plate, an archeologist would race up and snatch it and put it in a museum. The primitive people tried all kinds of schemes to protect their pots and plates, including burying them, but the archeologists would just dig them up. Finally, with nothing to cook in or eat from, the primitive people starved to death and became extinct.

The next big trend in art was painting, which was invented because wealthy people needed something to put on their walls. One famous painter, Michelangelo (first name, Buford), even painted on the ceiling. This was before the discovery of acoustical tiles. In those days, everybody painted the same subject, which was Mother and Child. That was a really popular item. Occasionally, an artist would try something different, such as Mother and Trowel, or Mother and Labrador Retriever, but they never sold.

After the Mother and Child Phase came the Enormous Naked Women Eating Fruit Phase, which was followed by the Just Plain Fruit with No Women of Any Kind Phase and the Famous Kings and Dukes Wearing Silly Outfits Phase. All of these phases were part of the Sharp and Clear School of painting, which means that even though the subjects were boring, they were at least recognizable. The Sharp and Clear School ended with Vincent Van Gogh, who invented the Fuzzy but Still Recognizable School and cut off his ear. This led to the No Longer Recognizable at All School, and finally to the Sharp and Clear Again but Mostly Just Rectangles School, which is the school that is popular today, except at shopping malls.

"He knows all about art, but he doesn't know what he likes."

"We all know that art is not truth. Art is a lie
that makes us realize truth."

— *Pablo Picasso*

BOSTON (AP) — The bizarre behavior and frenetic painting of
Vincent Van Gogh, the Dutch impressionist who cut off his ear,
probably resulted from an abnormality of the brain that has only
recently been recognized, a doctor says.

Van Gogh churned out hundreds of paintings in his last years of
life, sometimes finishing two masterpieces a day. He died after
shooting himself in the chest in 1890.

Dr. Shahram Khoshbin of Harvard Medical School says that Van
Gogh's relentless painting, aggression, and several other unusual
habits are all symptoms of a disturbance of the brain's temporal
lobe, which plays a role in memory, hearing and other functions.

Van Gogh's most productive time was the period during 1888-
1889 that he spent in Arles, France. Over 444 days, he painted
about 200 oils, made more than 100 drawings and watercolors and
wrote 200 letters. Among these were his most famous paintings —
his vibrantly colored sunflowers, fishing boats and country scenes.

It was, Khoshbin said, an outburst of hypergraphia. "When you
look at those paintings and realize that each one was done in a day,
you realize that it takes tremendous compulsion for someone to do
that."

Lincoln Star, June 8, 1985, p. 2. Reprinted by permission of The Associated Press.

"You know, the more I think about it, the more I realize that nothing is more truly artistic than to love people."

— *Vincent Van Gogh*

Vincent Van Gogh left almost 600 paintings in nine years of intense productivity. Among these works, "The Red Orchard" was unique. Why?

Need more clues? See page 146.

20
Tank U.

THE PLEDGE OF A LESION

Melancholy or apathy may follow in the wake of a nuclear war. Fight disorientation by reasserting your sense of national identity. Repeat *The Pledge of a Lesion*:

I pledge a lesion
to a conflagration
of the blighted state of America,
and to the repugnance
for which it stands;
one contamination
underground,
invisible,
with lithium and rubble for all.

Victor Langer and Walter Thomas, *The Nuclear War Fun Book* (New York: Holt, Rinehart and Winston, 1982), p. 118.

"War is not healthy for children and other living things."

— *Antiwar poster*

DOONESBURY

by Garry Trudeau

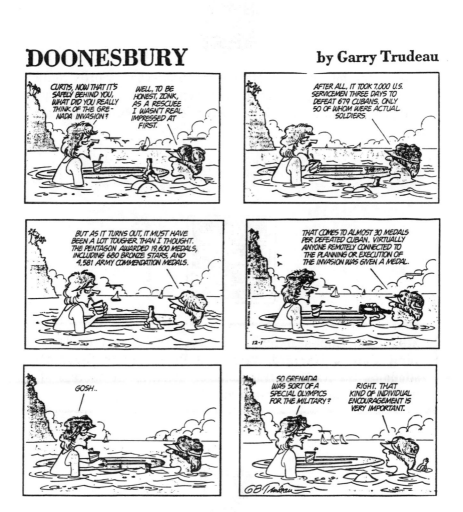

Dear Mrs, Mr, Miss, or Mr and Mrs Daneeka: Words cannot express the deep personal grief I experienced when your husband, son, father or brother was killed, wounded or reported missing in action.

Joseph Heller, *Catch-22*, 1961.

After much soul-searching, you have decided to turn down admission to Harvard, Yale, and Princeton in favor of attending the National War College. What is the address of this institution of higher mortality?

Need more clues? See page 147.

21
Math According to Miss Margarida

Why can't you divide by zero?

I can and often do divide by zero, but only after I've made the necessary preparations. First of all, I fast for forty-eight hours, consuming during that time only mildly fluoridated water. Next I don my special Mylar/Teflon division-by-zero suit. Then I put on a digitally recorded compact disc of Gregorian chants and begin with dividing very small numbers by other very small numbers. As the numbers get smaller, the sparks begin to fly. If all goes well, I take a deep breath and divide a very small number by zero. There's a flash of light, a muffled roar, and when I come to, the lab is filled with smoke and the scent of burning Mylar. So you see, you can divide by zero if you really want to. But chances are you just don't want to badly enough.

— Dr. Science

Dr. Science with Rodney, *The Official Dr. Science Big Book of Science* (Chicago: Contemporary Books, Inc., 1986), pp. 114-115. Reprinted from THE OFFICIAL DR. SCIENCE BIG BOOK OF SCIENCE © 1986 by Duck's Breath, used with permission of Contemporary Books, Inc., Chicago.

Education is a serious business! You are here to learn. Do you know what mathematics is? Of course not! In the eighth grade and you don't know a thing about mathematics! I'm going to teach you a few instances. Division. Now, to divide means that each one of you want to get more than the others. Do you understand? I am going to teach you on the blackboard to make it perfectly clear. Let us suppose the following problem. In this classroom there are only twelve bananas for thirty-five students. Now, pay attention please. These thirty-five mouths wanting bananas must therefore divide the twelve bananas among themselves. What is going to happen? Well, the strongest student will get eight or nine bananas all for himself. The second strongest will get three or four bananas. And the thirty-three remaining mouths will be left perfectly without bananas. That is division.

Roberto Athayde, *Miss Margarida's Way* (Garden City, NY: Nelson Doubleday, Inc., 1977), pp. 11-12.

"Yes! we have no bananas — we have no bananas today."

If you find math according to Miss Margarida slippery, then try to explain this: In thin lens theory, what is the center of the circle of least confusion?

Need more clues? See pages 148-149.

22
Time After Time

DETROIT (AP) — Outdated teaching methods have produced a generation of college students with a dangerous ignorance of geography that could lead to a repetition of past errors, says the head of the National Geographic Society.

"I'm suggesting that ignorance kills, and I'm suggesting that if you are ignorant, you aren't going very far in the world," Gilbert M. Grosvenor, the fifth of his family to lead the society, said Monday.

A knowledge of geography would have taught American leaders in the 1960s that "the artificial boundaries of Vietnam that split across strong tribes would not work," Grosvenor told the Economic Club of Detroit as part of the 81st annual meeting of the Association of American Geographers. "An 'F' in geography obviously triggered our original involvement."

Grosvenor cited examples of geographic ignorance:

A survey of one university found that 95 percent of the newly enrolled freshmen could not point out Vietnam on a map.

In a Dallas secondary school, 20 percent of the children faced with a globe and asked to point out the United States put their country in Brazil.

Lincoln Journal, April 23, 1985, p. 3. Reprinted with permission of The Associated Press.

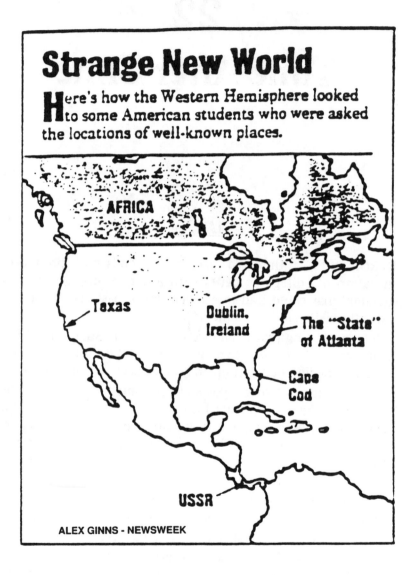

Strange New World

Here's how the Western Hemisphere looked to some American students who were asked the locations of well-known places.

AFRICA

Texas

Dublin, Ireland

The "State" of Atlanta

Cape Cod

USSR

ALEX GINNS - NEWSWEEK

Newsweek, September 1, 1986, p. 67. Used with permission of NEWSWEEK.

I know this is a lot to be telling you. But I know nothing about maps. I mean absolutely nothing, not one thing. I don't know where the U.S. or L.A. or Calif. is located...I don't know the difference between countries, cities, town's *(sic)*, or states. Can I have a little of your help please?

A note from a California 10th grader to his teacher, *Newsweek*, September 1, 1986, p. 67.

"I have seen the future and it is a place about 70 miles east of here where it is lighter...."
— *Laurie Anderson*

John and Jane live on a planet that is 8,000 miles in diameter hurtling through space at 1,800 miles a second, tipped 23 1/2° to the plane of its orbit. What chance does their love have?

Mark O'Donnell, *Elementary Education* (Boston: Faber and Faber, 1985), p. 38.

"When American men were asked, 'Have you had any sexual thoughts in the last five minutes?' thirty-seven percent said 'yes.' In Ghana, sixty-five percent answered 'yes.' How many time zones does a resident of Denver, Colorado need to travel through to reach Ghana?"

Teachers: A Survival Guide for the Grown-Up in the Classroom by Art Peterson, (New York: Plume/New American Library, 1985), p. 80.

Need more clues? See page 150.

23

Don't Play It Again, Sam

"Chapter One. He adored New York City, although to him, it was a metaphor for the decay of contemporary culture. How hard it was to exist in a society desensitized by drugs, loud music, television, crime, garbage." Too angry. I don't wanna be angry. "Chapter One. He was as...tough and romantic as the city he loved. Behind his black-rimmed glasses was the coiled sexual power of a jungle cat." I love this. "New York was his town. And it always would be."

Woody Allen, *Four Films of Woody Allen* (New York: Random House, 1982), p. 182.
"Manhattan" screenplay by Woody Allen and Marshall Brickman.

ALVY: There's an old joke. Uh, two elderly women are at a Catskills mountain resort, and one of 'em says: "Boy, the food at this place is really terrible." The other one says, "Yeah, I know, and such...small portions." Well, that's essentially how I feel about life. Full of loneliness and misery and suffering and unhappiness, and it's all over much too quickly. The — the other important joke for me is one that's, uh, usually attributed to Groucho Marx, but I think it appears originally in Freud's wit and its relation to the unconscious. And it goes like this — I'm paraphrasing: Uh..."I would never wanna belong to any club that would have someone like me for a member." That's the key joke of my adult life and in terms of my relationships with women. Tsch, you know, lately the strangest things have been going through my mind, 'cause I turned forty, tsch, and I guess I'm going through a life crisis or something, I don't know. I, uh...and I'm not worried about aging. I'm not one o' those characters, you know. Although I'm balding slightly on top, that's about the worst you can say about me. I, uh, I think I'm gonna get better as I get older, you know? I think I'm gonna be the — the balding virile type, you know, as opposed to say the, uh, distinguished gray, for instance, you know? 'Less I'm neither o' those two. Unless I'm one o' those guys with saliva dribbling out of his mouth who wanders into a cafeteria with a shopping bag screaming about socialism.

From STAN MACK'S OUT-TAKES by Stan Mack, copyright © 1976-1984 by Stan Mack. Published by the Overlook Press, Lewis Hollow Road, Woodstock, New York. $12.95 (cloth), $7.95 (paper).

...[This film] is a curious olio of nightclub patter, revue sketches and one-liners, most of them quite funny but uneasily stitched together. What comes out resembles a movie only as something midway between a crazy quilt and a potato resembles a suit of clothes. This sort of film wears thin too easily, laughter that is largely pointless becomes in the end exhausting. This does not necessarily happen within a single Woody Allen film, which, kept wisely short, can generally squeeze by without our realizing until later that we have been exercising our jaws in a vacuum — that we could have gotten roughly the same effect from laughing gas, sneezing powder or a mutual tickling session with a friendly prankster.

— John Simon

In the review quoted above, which Woody Allen film is Mr. Simon panning?

Need more clues? See pages 151-152.

24
And the Beat
Goes On...

like
there's this underage chick...
suzuki beane...
a beat baby if there ever was one
she shares a pad with
her poet father
and sculptress mother
like
suzuki writes poetry too...
real crazy...
and has to go to school,
which is a drag...
like there's this teacher,
miss shoemaker, who says,
like is no word
to begin a sentence with.

Sandra Scoppettone, *Suzuki Beane* (New York: Doubleday & Co., 1961).

Suzuki Beane's fictional father

Drawing by Louise Fitzhugh from *Suzuki Beane* by Sandra Scoppettone (New York: Doubleday & Co., 1961).

Some people say, "like, kids say 'like' like too much" because we're like insecure and like are like totally afraid that people like won't like us. But like, that's totally like wrong! Like, I don't like say "like" like all the time. That would be, like, totally, like, annoying. Like, you'd think I like didn't have anything like important to say.

— *Grace MacNamee, age 15*
(for a Milton Academy essay assignment on "Parody").

> "I saw the best minds of my generation
> destroyed by madness."
> — *Allen Ginsberg*

See
    It was like this when

        we waltz into this place
a couple of Papish cats
      is doing an Aztec two-step

And I says
    Dad let's cut
but then this dame
      comes up behind me see
      and says
      You and me could really exist

Wow I says
    Only the next day
    she has bad teeth
    and really hates
    poetry

© Seth Feinberg — "No Danger to the Public" Postcards.

"But then they danced down the streets like dingledodies and I shambled after as I've been doing all my life after people who interest me, because the only people for me are the mad ones, the ones who are mad to live, mad to talk, mad to be saved, desirous of everything at the same time, the ones who never yawn or say a commonplace thing, but burn, burn, burn like fabulous yellow roman candles exploding like spiders across the stars and in the middle you see the blue centerlight pop and everybody goes 'Awww!'"

— *Jack Kerouac*

Lawrence Ferlinghetti is generally considered to be the most popular of the Beat poets. The Beat movement came to public attention in 1956 with the publication of what two works of literature?

Need more clues? See page 153.

25
Kowa Bonga!

There was no greater honor for a child whose parents had
bought one of those new television sets in the late forties and early
fifties than to be a member of Howdy Doody's Peanut Gallery. But
most kids who resided in or were visiting New York City, the real
"Hollywood" of TV in those days, could only dream of attending a
live telecast of Howdy Doody and seeing in person the friendly host
Buffalo Bob Smith, the mischievous yet lovable clown Clarabell, and
myriad other characters with such colorful names as Dilly Dally, the
Featherman and Mr. Bluster. Almost every child in the United
States faced the same problem when it came to writing for tickets to
be a part of the Peanut Gallery on Howdy Doody. The waiting list
for tickets was several years long.

Howdy Doody's Peanut Gallery was the show's studio audience, composed of the luckiest kids in the world. Not only were they lucky because of the free balloons, loaf of Wonder Bread and tube of Colgate Dental Cream which was given to every one of them, but mostly because they were among the privileged minority who would actually see the juvenile world's number one television idol, Howdy Doody himself....

Buffalo Bob Smith, dressed in his familiar yellow outfit with red fringe and buffalo insignia, would shout enthusiastically, "Say, kids, what time is it?!"

The Peanut Gallery, and the shut-in members watching the program at home, would shriek deafeningly the most quoted line of any children's television show:

"It's Howdy Doody time!!!"

IT'S HOWDY DOODY TIME

What's this? Another American pop idol goes big time? Beginning this month, the image of Howdy Doody, the freckle-faced puppet with the matted red hair, will appear on cookie jars, mugs, lamps, pens and night shirts. King Features Syndicate, the Hearst Corp. unit in charge of licensing the character, expects the '50s TV star will bring in the bucks much the way Betty Boop, Popeye and Blondie have. So far, 20 manufacturers have signed on to peddle Howdy Doody wares.

HOWDY DOODY

Boston Globe, "Extras," May 31, 1988, p. 61. Reprinted courtesy of The Boston Globe.

What character on the Howdy Doody Show would exclaim "Kowa Bonga!"?

Need more clues? See pages 154-155.

PART TWO

The Clues

1
Assessing the SAT

IS THIS TEST TOO TOUGH?

A few enlightened people believe prospective college football players should meet the same admission requirements that regular students meet. To that end, a friend has sent us what he swears is a confidential entrance exam developed by a major southern state university that assures future Saturday heroes will have brains as well as brawn. A few sample questions follow.

Can you guess the animal in this incomplete drawing?

START

FINISH

Get through the maze.

Connect the dots.

Find the aardvark hiding in the back of the pickup.

Illustrations for SPORTS ILLUSTRATED by Patrick McDonnell © 1986.

Every state with an average of math and verbal SAT scores of 510 or above also had an average high temperature in January of less than 42 degrees.

Patrice Horn, "California," *Psychology Today*, March 1983, p. 77.

LSAT *L*aw *S*chool *A*ptitude *T*est. An examination required for admission to law school and consisting of questions such as the following:

Directions: Read the following passage and blacken the space beside the answer you believe is most nearly correct.

"It was the best of times, it was the worst of times, it was the age of wisdom, it was the age of foolishness...[read the novel *A Tale of Two Cities*, attached to your exam booklet]...it is a far, far better test that I go to than I have ever known."

Question: In the above story, what time is it?

☐ (a) The best of times.
☐ (b) The worst of times.
☐ (c) The *New York Times*.
☐ (d) About two o'clock.

A. You know the author, Ernest Boyer, and you know the text, "The Carnegie Foundation Report on Secondary Education in America." You don't need a high school diploma to decide what to do next.

B. Stop. Put your pencils down. Close your booklet and wait for further instructions.

Still can't find the answer? See page 159.

2

Ask Not...

"A child miseducated is a child lost."

— John F. Kennedy

SHOE by Jeff MacNelly

Reprinted by permission: Tribune Media Services.

A. Sometimes in the course of human events, it becomes necessary to bear any burden, pay any price, meet any hardship, nay, even use microfilm.

B. All the news that's fit to print often fits into the next day's paper.

Still can't find the answer? See page 160.

3

Nerds and Knotheads

"Oh, boy! The 'Nerd'! ... Now
my collection's complete!"

Reprinted by permission of UFS, Inc.

"His slang...was always a little out of date as though he had studied a dictionary of popular usage, but not in the latest edition."

— *Graham Greene,* The Comedians

A. Don't be a knothead. Words are defined in word dictionaries. Slang words are defined in slang dictionaries.

B. Phooey.

Still can't find the answer? See page 161.

4

Mall-Adjusted

"If you think the United States has stood still,
who built the largest shopping mall
in the world?"

— *Richard Nixon*

A. We can find this reference book in world record time.
B. Shop 'til you drop.

Still can't find the answer? See page 162.

5

Back in the U.S.S.R.

"A Soviet woman without a man is like a fish
without a tractor."

— *Randall McCutcheon* (with apologies to Gloria Steinem)

Jeff Danziger in *The Christian Science Monitor* © 1988 TCSPS.

"Never face the facts."

— *Ruth Gordon*

"Facts are useless in emergencies."

— *David Byrne*

Illustration by Dana Fradon in *Insincerely Yours* (New York: Charles Scribners, 1978). Reprinted by permission of John Hawkins and Assoc.

A. Can't read Russian? No problem. Consult the reference in English that summarizes what is reported in more than 50 foreign and U.S. newspapers and magazines. So when you want the facts (or what passes for the facts), look there first.

B. Nyet! No more clues! The authors have a "collective" headache.

Still can't find the answer? See page 163.

6

It Must Be Love

"We had the perfect second-grade romance. I liked him and he copied my math."

— Dawn Clendenen, age 14,
Valley High School, West Des Moines

KUDZU by permission of Doug Marlette and Creators Syndicate, Inc.

"There's no money in poetry, but there's no
poetry in money either."

— *Robert Graves*

A. Do not wander lonely as a cloud. Instead, search for a poetry reference that indexes first lines. Believe it or not, there is one. Now you have taken the road less traveled by, and that will make all the difference.

B. This question may seem to be without rhyme or reason — but tracking down the answer will be a picnic.

Still can't find the answer? See page 164.

7

Bach-Analia

Peanuts/By Charles Schulz

Reprinted by permission of UFS, Inc.

"If music be the breakfast food of love, kindly
do not disturb until lunch time."

— *James Agee*

A. Even if you have Van Gogh's ear for music (see Question 19, "Gogh For It"), you must realize that you need a reference that lists all of J.S. Bach's works.

B. A final note: Be sharp!

Still can't find the answer? See page 165.

8

Ducks in the Wry

"Asking a working writer what he thinks
about critics is like asking a lamp post what it
feels about dogs."

— *John Osborne*

A. You can either thumb through every *San Francisco Chronicle* printed since *The Catcher in the Rye* came out (unless, of course, you have access to the *Chronicle's* index), OR you can look for a reference including major reviews of books printed during their first year of publication.
B. As Holden once said, "Don't ever tell anybody anything. If you do, you start missing everybody."

Still can't find the answer? See page 166.

9

A Goldberg Variation

First it was Whoopi Cushion. Then it was French, like Whoopi Cushon. My mother said, "Nobody's gonna respect you with a name like that." So I put Goldberg on it. Goldberg's a part of my family somewhere and that's all I can say about it.

Whoopi Goldberg, from an interview with David Remnick published in the *Washington Post*, December 25, 1984.

A. If you know what's what, you won't go to *Who's Who*. Find, instead, a current reference with well-documented biographical articles.

B. "I am my show." (Whoopi Goldberg)

Still can't find the answer? See page 167.

10

Much Ado About Everything

"It is a good thing for an uneducated man to
read books of quotations."

— *Winston Churchill*

A. What you need is a violent brainstorm — a sort of tempest of
the temporal lobes, as it were.

B. Shakespeare and Bartlett's...what a pear.

Still can't find the answer? See page 168.

11

Rated R

SEX IN MOVIES.

SEX IN ROCK LYRICS.

SEX ON TV.

SEX IN ADVERTISING.

CONTRACEPTIVES IN SCHOOL—

TO PROTECT US FROM THE SEX EDUCATION WE GET IN THE MEDIA.

Jules Feiffer, *Feiffer's Children* (New York: Andrews, McMeel & Parker, 1986),
p. 47. Copyright © Universal Press Syndicate. Used by permission.

"If S-E-X ever rears its ugly head, close your
eyes before you see the rest of it."

— *Alan Ayckbourn,* Bedroom Farce

A. The day before the film premiered in New York City, the first American birth control clinic opened. Both were firsts. Find a reference that marks such birth-shattering, cloth-tattering events.

B. You know when the film premiered. You can guess what the film was missing. Find a reference that indexes "first" events by dates and subjects.

Still can't find the answer? See page 169.

12

A Conscientious Objection

"Any man more right than his neighbors
constitutes a majority of one."

— *Henry David Thoreau*

Reprinted by permission of *Mark Twain Journal*.

A. The day after the day that lives on in infamy.

B. Congressional records were made to be broken.

Still can't find the answer? See page 170.

13

Oliver Twisted

"There are three types of lies — lies, damned lies, and statistics."

— *Mark Twain*

"Meaningless statistics were up one-point-five percent this month over last month."

Illustration by Dana Fradon in *Insincerely Yours* (New York: Charles Scribners, 1978). Reprinted by permission of John Hawkins and Assoc.

A. Like an orphan, you're on your own. But there *is* one thing you can count on, one place you can go: a "home" for statistics.

B. Such a place really exists. And we're not Fagin it.

Still can't find the answer? See page 171.

14

Gobble Gobble Glup Glup

> "When I use a word," Humpty Dumpty said in rather a scornful tone, "it means just what I choose it to mean — neither more nor less."
>
> — *Lewis Carroll,* Alice in Wonderland

A. People aren't the only ones to go through "phrases." Find a reference book that does the same.

B. Amokraker — n. One who writes for the *National Enquirer.*

Still can't find the answer? See page 172.

15

Days of Our Lives

"Mush, you huskies!"

— Sergeant Preston of the Yukon

A. Happy days are here again...because months have days, and some days have books.

B. So fur, so good.

Still can't find the answer? See page 173.

16

Moo-Goo-Gai-Panic

"I don't mind 800 million Chinese drinking a bottle of Coca-Cola a day, but I don't want them to bring back the empties."

— *Art Buchwald*

"Well, if I called the wrong number, why did you answer the phone?"

"If the phone doesn't ring, it's me."
— *Jimmy Buffet*

GEORGIA POWER—

Customer Service
165 E. Dougherty St..353-1121
Accounting Inquiries
165 E. Dougherty St..353-1121
Application for Service
165 E. Dougherty St..353-1121
Bill Payment
165 E. Dougherty St..353-1121
Marketing Representation
165 E. Dougherty St..353-1121
Division Office
1001 Prince Av..353-1121
If No Answer..353-1121

—Athens, Ga., telephone directory

The number you have reached is not a working number. Please hang up and forget it.

The New Yorker, December 28, 1987, p. 103.

A. If you go to the card catalog and look up "Chinese restaurants" you'll get a wrong number.

B. Let your fingers do the walking to a reference that includes phone directories.

Still can't find the answer? See page 174.

17

One Small Stumble

"In the space age the most important space
is between the ears."

— *Ann Armstrong*

A. If you look up "moon," all you'll probably find is *"see* Green Cheese."

B. Don't believe everything you read.

Still can't find the answer? See page 175.

18

You Can Bet on It

"How much would you pay for all the secrets of the universe? Wait, don't answer yet. You also get this six-quart covered combination spaghetti pot and clam steamer. Now how much would you pay?"

The More the Merrier: Cartoons by Michael Maslin (New York: Simon & Schuster/Fireside, 1987), p. 45. Reprinted by permission of Simon & Schuster, Inc.

"You can observe a lot just by watching."

— Yogi Berra

A. If you don't think "business," strike one.
B. If you don't think "periodical," strike two.
C. If you don't think periodically, you're already out of business.

Still can't find the answer? See page 176.

19

Gogh for It

KUDZU   by Doug Marlette

EVERYTHING I SAY TO
VINCENT GOES IN ONE
EAR...

KUDZU by permission of Doug Marlette and Creators Syndicate, Inc.

"One may have a blazing hearth in one's soul,
and yet no one ever comes to sit by it."

— *Vincent Van Gogh*

A.   Lend me your ear. Although there are many places to go for this answer, one in particular is especially useful. If you don't look for a reference that indexes paintings by title, then you're not thinking still, and perhaps you never will.

B.   Most researchers do not have starry nights. It seems as if they're *always* in the dark.

Still can't find the answer? See page 177.

20

Tank U.

> "Education is not nearly as sudden as a massacre, but in the long run it is more deadly."
>
> — *Mark Twain*

Join The Army
Travel To Exotic Places
Meet Unusual People
And Kill Them

A. All's fair in love and war college...if only you knew where to find them.

B. At ease. The address is in the *Congressional Directory*.

C. "Golly!" (Gomer Pyle)

Still can't find the answer? See page 178.

21

Math According to Miss Margarida

"I don't believe in mathematics."
— *Albert Einstein*

A. Silberberg, *SPY*, June 1988, p. 28. Reprinted by permission of UFS, Inc.

A. Don't focus on the confusion. Think thin... *lens.*

B. Take a calculated risk. Find a mathematics reference that "lens" itself to photography.

C. If you suspect that there's something in this question that doesn't add up, you're right.

Still can't find the answer? See page 179.

22

Time After Time

"For time is the longest distance
between two places."

— *Tennessee Williams,* The Glass Menagerie

"Time is not the only compromise."

— *Ferron* (Canadian folksinger)

A. Facts are found in almanacs. Illustrations of facts are found in atlases.

B. You need a map that includes Ghana, Colorado, and the time zones between them. If you do not have such a map, your hopes for solving this question will be Ghana with the wind.

Still can't find the answer? See page 180.

23

Don't Play It Again, Sam

"Let me see now... Would that be under 'F' for 'film,' or 'P' for 'picture,' or 'M' for 'motion picture,' or 'S' for 'sound,' or..."

Schmidt, *Phi Delta Kappan*, April 1975, p. 538.

> ## "If my film makes one more person miserable, I'll feel I've done my job."
>
> — *Woody Allen*

A. Mr. Simon is full of literary criticism for his contemporary, Mr. Allen. Find a reference that is literally overflowing with the same.

B. Simon says, "Don't buy a ticket." Don't listen to Simon. Don't play silly games.

Still can't find the answer? See page 181.

24

And the Beat Goes On...

"Walking on water wasn't built in a day."
— *Jack Kerouac*

A. Don't worry. Everything's copacetic. The writers of the Beat generation were significant contributors to American literature.

B. There's a real cool encyclopedia that provides information on writers and writing in America. Wow!

C. Splitsville!

Still can't find the answer? See page 182.

25

Kowa Bonga!

"Say, kids...what time is it?"
— *Buffalo Bob*

A. Fred Flintstone, Herman Munster, Hawkeye Pierce, Mr. Ed....Every serious couch potato has his T.V. heroes.

B. Well, that's enough from the peanut gallery!

Still can't find the answer? See page 183.

PART THREE

The
Answers

1

Assessing the SAT

The new assessment test for students recommended by "The Carnegie Foundation Report on Secondary Education in America" would be called the "Student Achievement and Advisement Test," or SAAT.

The answer may be found in *High School: A Report on Secondary Education in America* by Ernest Boyer (New York: Harper & Row, 1983, © Carnegie Foundation for the Advancement of Teaching), p. 133.

Boyer explains: "The goal of the new assessment program would be to evaluate the academic achievement of the student — linking it to the core curriculum that the student studied. The goal also would be to provide advisement, helping students make decisions more intelligently about their futures — again, not to screen students out of options but to help them move on with confidence to college and to jobs.

"The College Board now offers achievement tests in specific subject areas. With some modification, these could form the basis for at least the achievement portion of the new evaluation program. The National Assessment for Educational Progress also offers a model for the type of evaluation we propose. Further, we are encouraged that the College Board recently has released a thoughtful report on what a college-bound high school student should know. This provides a beginning, we believe, for the linking of education and evaluation.

"This new assessment instrument would be only one part of a larger, more comprehensive student evaluation program. The full assessment program should include carefully constructed teacher evaluations, student-prepared portfolios containing academic and vocational work samples, a student interest inventory, as well as a Senior Independent Project."

2

Ask Not...

The end of the quotation reads, "...probably the greatest concentration of talent and genius in this house except for perhaps those times when Thomas Jefferson ate alone."

The answer is found in the *New York Times* (April 30, 1962), p. 1, col. 5. If you paid attention to Clue B, you probably looked there first.

If you didn't, you could have turned to *The New York Times Index* (New York: New York Times Company; published semimonthly, quarterly, and annually). You might have checked volume 50, the 1962 annual edition (since that was the year of the dinner, as noted in the question). And if you looked first under "Kennedy" and then under "Social Functions," you would have found what you were looking for on page 524.

According to *The New York Times Guide to Reference Materials* (Revised Edition) by Mona McCormick (New York: Signet/New American Library, 1971), *The New York Times Index* is "useful in locating items in your local papers (except, of course, strictly local interest events) because it establishes dates." The *Guide* states that the index can also be used as a reference itself without referring to a particular newspaper: "Major news stories are given brief summaries in the index, and the entries are listed chronologically under the subject, so the course of events is clearly seen."

The best advice we can give you for the future is to first study the "instructive page" that appears in each issue of *The New York Times Index*. Then begin your research.

3

Nerds and Knotheads

The word "knothead" was first used by Max Shulman in his *Collection of Campus Stories: The Many Loves of Dobie Gillis* (Garden City, NY: Garden City Books, 1953), p. 61. To quote: "Look at Petey — a knothead...."

The answer may be found in the *Dictionary of American Slang, Second Supplemented Edition*, compiled by Harold Wentworth and Stuart Berg Flexner (New York: Thomas Y. Crowell Company, 1975), p. 310. (Look directly to the right of this entry and you can learn about the origins of "knucklehead," too.)

You may be a greenie to the art of research, and you may think that only schleps or sickniks get wigged out by reading a blat, but you will be a yo-yo, a schlemiel, or a kluck if you try to fake it on your next research paper or just zizz off in class. Your grade will probably bite the dust and, most likely, you will never be a whiz kid.

If the preceding paragraph seems incoherent, then consult the *Dictionary of American Slang*. The preface states that it "points out who uses slang and what 'flavor' it conveys." It contains "as large and representative body of American slang as possible, some colloquialisms, cant, jargon, argot and idioms frequently used in popular novels and movies."

Now isn't that just jim-dandy?

4

Mall-Adjusted

The world's largest shopping mall is the West Edmonton Mall, located in West Edmonton, Alberta, Canada.

The answer may be found in the *Guinness Book of World Records* (New York: Sterling Publishing Co., 1962-date). We found it on page 344 in the 1988 edition after looking in the Index under "Shopping Centers."

Writing about this teenage wasteland for the December, 1986 *Smithsonian* magazine (pages 35-42), William Severini Kowinski went on to say, "To begin to put its size into perspective, consider that the previous record holder as the largest mall was the Del Amo complex in southern California. West Edmonton is twice its size. Fashioned from two existing malls, Del Amo has 360 stores. West Edmonton added 400 stores just in its recently completed Phase III, for a total exceeding 800. That's 11 major department stores, more than 110 eating places, 200 stores that sell women's clothing (35 for men) and 50 shoe stores. The mall also has several theme shopping areas, the Ice Palace skating rink, a Spanish galleon in its own lake, four submarines, and 37 animal displays and a petting zoo — birds, Siberian tiger cubs, miniature Arabian horses, reindeer, baby bears, baby moose and one baby elephant."

The Guinness Book of World Records, as it boasts in the preface, is the top-selling copyright book in publishing history. And who can blame them for bragging? They should be proud to publicize information about the man who can smoke 38 pipes simultaneously, the single largest serving of mashed potatoes, and the world record for worm charming.

5

Back in the U.S.S.R.

Tass described the classes as consisting of "conversations on friendship and love, marriage and family life, [and the] physiological-hygienic aspects of mutual relations of young people."

The answer may be found in the January 1985 *Facts on File* (New York: Facts on File, 1940 to date), pp. 171-172. First, however, you should have gone to the *Facts on File Index* — "your key to subjects, people, organizations, countries, and U.S. companies covered in the *Facts on File News Digest* articles."

According to Bruce L. Felknor, author of *How To Look Things Up and Find Things Out* (New York: William Morrow, 1988), *Facts on File* is "a reliable compendium of current events kept relentlessly up to date...to find or verify facts fast...actually, the service is a weekly pamphlet of concise summaries of developments in a wide range of fields, from world affairs to sports and the arts. Each page is a grid, with numbered meridians and lettered latitude markers, so the index can send the reader at once to that column inch on the page where the desired information lurks."

6

It Must Be Love

The title of this poem is "The Picnic," and the name of the poet is John Logan. It was published in his book *Only the Dreamer Can Change the Dream.*

The answer may be found in *Granger's Index to Poetry,* 8th edition, edited by William F. Bernhardt (New York: Columbia University Press, 1986), p. 584.

This standard reference work includes author, subject, title, AND first line indexes. Its purpose, as stated in the Preface, is "to assist the reader in identifying and locating poems or selections from poems appearing in most generally accessible anthologies."

As you wander through *Granger's,* you will find references to other poems that may plant the seeds of curiosity — like "Ode to a Pig while His Nose Was Being Bored," "Elegy for the Monastery Barn," and "Cupid the Ploughboy." Entries in the Subject Index range from Civil War to Christmas cards, from funerals to furniture.

In the Author Index (to the 7th edition, which many libraries may still have), one can discover that "So This Is Nebraska" is one of the many poems by Ted Kooser. A poem with an immediate, if somewhat subtle, pronoun reference problem.

7

Bach-Analia

The answer is 1734-1735.

The answer may be found in *The New Grove Dictionary of Music and Musicians* by Sir George Grove (1820-1900), edited by Stanley Sadie (London: MacMillan Publishers Ltd., 1980), volume I (of a 20-volume dictionary), p. 825.

Grove's *Dictionary* hath charms to soothe even the savage researcher. According to *The New York Times Guide to Reference Materials,* "it covers the whole field of music from 1450 on and includes musical and related terms such as 'boffo' and subjects like the Berkshire festivals, music history, theory and practice, and musical instruments. Bibliographies are given, and the complete catalogs of works by major musicians."

NOTE: Other reference works disagree with these dates. The second edition of the *Harvard Dictionary of Music,* for example, claims that the *Coffee Cantata* was composed in 1732. See for yourself by checking the *Harvard Dictionary,* edited by Willi Apel (Cambridge, MA: The Belknap Press of Harvard University Press, 1972), p. 181.

From 1732 to 1735, even for Bach, is a long coffee break.

8

Ducks in the Wry

Lewis Vogler wrote this review, which appeared on page 17 of the *San Francisco Chronicle* on July 15, 1951.

To find the answer, you should have gone first to the card catalog to find out when *The Catcher in the Rye* was published — 1951. This would have been your starting point when looking through *Book Review Digest* (New York: Wilson, 1905 to date), which excerpts selected reviews of new books in their publication years. (Vogler's review is excerpted on page 772 in the issue of *Book Review Digest* that covers March 1951-February 1952.)

Along the way, you might also have found reviews of C.N. Robinson's *Meet the Plastics* (another "Graduate," perhaps?); H. Kuhn's *Encounter with Nothingness* (the lighter side of existentialism); and Johnny Farrell's *If I Were In Your Golf Shoes* (illustrated with 18 — count them — action photographs). Good stuff, eh?

9

A Goldberg Variation

Whoopi was "tired of working on living people who all wanted to look like Farrah Fawcett."

The answer may be found in the *Current Biography Yearbook,* volume 46, for 1985 (New York: H.W. Wilson, 1985), p. 145.

Current Biography, issued monthly and then published as an annual cumulated volume, contains "brief, objective, accurate, and well-documented biographical articles about living leaders in all fields of human accomplishment the world over." Including their lives, their loves, their successes, their failures, and their accounts of how they starved and struggled or just got lucky.

Unlike *Who's Who, Current Biography* details both positive and negative information about the biographees. It asserts that "sketches have been made as accurate and objective as possible through careful researching." A good policy for all of us.

10

Much Ado About Everything

The quotation is from Act I, scene ii of William Shakespeare's play *The Tempest*.

The answer may be found in *Familiar Quotations* by John Bartlett, Fifteenth Edition, edited by Emily Morison Beck (Boston: Little, Brown, and Co., 1980), p. 247.

Bartlett's *Familiar Quotations* contains "passages, phrases, and proverbs traced to their sources in ancient and modern literature." It even includes Ralph Waldo Emerson's quotation, "I hate quotations. Tell me what you know."

This book is useful in showing others exactly what you do know, with a little help from your quotable friends. Bartlett's is arranged chronologically by author and includes a key-word index. The quotation in the question can be found by looking in the index under "knowing," "loved," "books," "furnished," "library," "volumes," "prize," or "dukedom."

NOTE: Although Bartlett's is considered to be the standard collection of quotations, we recommend more contemporary collections for everyday use. See pages 187-191 for suggestions.

11

Rated R

The answer is "A Daughter of the Gods."

The answer may be found in *Famous First Facts* by Joseph Nathan Kane, 4th edition (New York: H.W. Wilson, 1981), p. 403.

This staple of reference collections is useful when researching the "first" of anything. The first electric tattoo machine, the first glue factory (a moment of silence for Mr. Ed), and even the first brawl in Congress — Matthew Lyon of Vermont had an argument with Roger Griswold of Connecticut and spat in Griswold's face — are all noted in this book, a "record of first happenings, discoveries, and inventions in American history." It contains 9,000 firsts arranged alphabetically by subject, plus four indexes (years, days of the month, personal names, geographical) to aid the researcher.

But we still wonder, "Who's on first?"

12

A Conscientious Objection

Her name was Jeanette Rankin, and she was a Representative from Montana. The answer is found on page 9537 of the *Congressional Record* for 1941.

To find the answer, you should have looked first at the *Congressional Record Index: Proceedings and Debates of Congress,* published biweekly (Washington, D.C.: U.S. Government Printing Office, 1873-present). Or since you know when the vote was cast (December 8, 1941), you could have pulled out the 1941 volume and turned to the speeches given on that date.

According to the *Subject Guide to U.S. Government Reference Sources* (Littleton, CO: Libraries Unlimited, Inc., 1985), the *Congressional Record* "contains the record of debates and pro- ceedings in Congress, messages to Congress, and records of voting. Users should be aware that speeches and debates are not necessarily verbatim. Members may edit and alter their remarks, or insert remarks without actually presenting them on the floor of Congress. A black bullet designates speeches that were inserted into the Record without having been delivered on the floor. However, absence of the bullet does not necessarily mean that the whole speech was actually delivered on the floor; only the first few sentences may have been read aloud."

The Subject and Name index to the *Congressional Record* includes a History of Bills and Resolutions section, arranged by bill number, which leads to information on all stages of bills from introduction to passage or defeat.

Spend a few hours wading through the murky waters of Congressional testimony and you will begin to agree with Will Rogers, who observed, "If the opposite of pro is con, then the opposite of progress is Congress."

13

Oliver Twisted

In 1982, there were 43,000 American children under age 18 who had been "full" orphans.

The answer may be found in *Statistical Abstract of the United States* (Washington, D.C.: U.S. Department of Commerce, Bureau of the Census; published annually). In the 108th edition (published in 1988), we found it on page 357.

Statistical Abstract of the United States, published since 1878, is a "standard summary of statistics on the social, political, and economic organization of the United States. It is designed to serve as a convenient volume for statistical reference and as a guide to other statistical publications and sources." If you like facts and figures, you'll find it fascinating.

Imagine numbers. Lots of them. And mingling with them, words and phrases grouped together in tables and charts. For example, you probably weren't aware that in 1984 the U.S. imported more smelt than anchovies and produced more pollock than haddock.

And "thanks to you" we donated more money to T.V. and radio service people than we did to the United Way. See how numbers work for all of us?

14

Gobble Gobble Glup Glup

If you wandered down the path of least resistance, then you probably picked up the nearest unabridged dictionary. This strategy may have produced a "correct" answer, but sometimes, dear researcher, correct is boring.

Thus, the need for the *Morris Dictionary of Word and Phrase Origins* (New York: Harper and Row, 1962), which is where you should have looked. According to the Morris, "amok" is derived from the Malayan word "amog." It goes on to state, "The word was originally used to describe the actions of Malayan tribesmen who, preoccupied by hatred and hashish, would rush furiously into hand-to-hand combat."

"Screaming meemies," "high mucky muck," and "sure as tunket," for example, aren't even mentioned in *Webster's Third New International Dictionary,* but they are discussed at length in the *Morris.* As the preface explains, this work deals "in depth and, if you will, in opinionated prose, with aspects of the language that the conventional dictionary must treat in conventional fashion."

15

Days of Our Lives

The Anchorage Fur Rendezvous is celebrated in February of each year. (Please note that this is a movable event.)

We found this answer in *The American Book of Days*, 3rd edition, by Jane M. Hatch (New York: H.W. Wilson Co., 1978), p. 176.

The American Book of Days "profiles the lives of many of the United States' distinguished citizens, explores the richness of its religious traditions, describes the variety of its holidays, customs and festivities, samples its folklore, and reports its ways — both solemn and fanciful — of marking anniversaries and commemorating achievements."

So why not celebrate the 200-year tradition of the "tar-tub" fires (February 22), the reenactment of Custer's Last Stand (observances and dates vary), or, better yet, the annual National Tom Sawyer Fence Painting Contest (on the Saturday nearest July 4).

Sometimes in research, as in life, a little whitewash goes a long way.

16

Moo-Goo-Gai-Panic

You could find the names and numbers of countless Peking restaurants in the *China Phone Book & Address Directory*, published by the China Phone Book Company Ltd., Box 11581, G.P.O., Hong Kong, Hong Kong.

To learn about this vast source of culinary possibilities, you should have consulted the *Directory of Directories*, 5th edition (Detroit: Gale Research Company, 1988). *The China Directory* is listed as item number 775 on page 132.

The *Directory of Directories*, according to its preface, "lists a wide range of domestic, foreign, and international publications, including general commercial and manufacturing directories; general and specialized lists of cultural institutions; directories of individual industries, trades, and professions; rosters of professional and scientific societies; and databases which have directory features." This reference is a handy tool for those who are interested in everything from Military Science to Mortuary Science (or are they the same thing?).

17

One Small Stumble

Time reported the quotation accurately on page 10 of its July 25, 1969 issue. However, the *Encyclopaedia Britannica* (fifteenth edition, 1987; *Micropaedia* Vol. I, under "Armstrong, Neil [Alden]" p. 574) corrected Mr. Armstrong's grammar. "Man" without a preceding article means not one man but man in general — mankind. *The Encyclopaedia's* editors apparently felt it necessary to correct Mr. Armstrong and changed his words to, "That's one small step for a man, one giant leap for mankind."

Time is indexed in the *Reader's Guide to Periodical Literature* (New York: H.W. Wilson Co., 1900-present). Every library has this popular reference tool. Even if they have no other reference works beyond bathroom graffiti, they have the *Reader's Guide*. Many beginning researchers gravitate there. Some never leave.

The *Reader's Guide* is a "cumulative author and subject index to periodicals of general interest published in the United States." One of its 200 "generally interesting" magazines indexed is, of course, *Time*.

If you need an explanation of *Time* magazine, our operators are standing by. Call our toll-free number, 1-800-(a-seven-letter-word-for-knothead). And if you order now, we'll send you, absolutely free, at no cost to anyone, our swimsuit issue (page after moldy page of green cheesecake).

18

You Can Bet on It

The answer is: 62% of the time.

The answer may be found in the article, "Betting on Baseball," by Ernie Kaufman, published in *Barron's* April 5, 1982 issue, p. 26.

Barron's is included in the *Business Periodicals Index* (New York: H.W. Wilson, 1958 to date). The source citation that should have led you to the answer is listed under both Ernie Kaufman and the subject heading, "Gambling."

According to the Prefatory Note in the *Business Periodicals Index*, "Subject fields indexed include accounting, advertising and public relations, banking, building and buildings, chemicals, communications, computer technology and applications, drugs and cosmetics, economics, electronics and electricity, finance and investments, industrial relations, insurance, international business, management and personnel administration, marketing, occupational health and safety, paper and pulp, petroleum and gas, printing and publishing, real estate, transportation, and other specific businesses, industries, and trades." For example, if you want to become a millionaire, in the carefully chosen words of *Forbes Magazine* (February 11, 1985), "There's plenty for everyone." You bet.

19

Gogh for It

"The Red Orchard" is the only painting by Van Gogh that was sold during the artist's lifetime.

This information may be found in many sources, but we recommend the *Encyclopedia of World Art*, edited by Bernard S. Meyers (New York: McGraw-Hill, 1959), vol. XIV, p. 698. We recommend this particular source because it indexes paintings by title.

The *Encyclopedia of World Art* includes everything from the unreal to the surreal. The preface states that its subject matter consists of "architecture, sculpture, and painting, and every other man-made object that, regardless of its purpose or technique, enters the field of esthetic judgment because of its form or decoration."

The New York Times Guide to Reference Materials suggests using the Index volume for finding "small topics within larger ones." For example, under the heading "Games and Toys" you can discover the "Esthetic consequences of play activities" (see vol. VI, p. 3) — for people who are Rambo-unctious.

20

Tank U.

The address, for your reference, is: Fort McNair, Fourth and P Streets, S.W., Washington, D.C. 20319-6000.

The answer may be found in the *Official 1987-1988 Congressional Directory* (Washington, D.C.: U.S. Government Printing Office, 1809-date), p. 810.

The New York Times Guide to Reference Materials describes the *Directory* as "an indispensable work containing information on congressional organizations and personnel."

The *Directory* lists the names and addresses of people, agencies, and institutions in the federal government. Learn exactly where your congressmen go to binge on junk food with the diagram of the Senate Snack Bar in the Capitol...discover the address, phone number and list of members of the International Pacific Halibut Commission, United States and Canada...find out the names of the children of Hawaii Senator Spark Matsunaga.

21

Math According to Miss Margarida

"The center of the circle of least confusion is the midpoint of the tangential and sagittal foci on a ray."

You may not understand that answer, but you could have found it in the *International Dictionary of Applied Mathematics*, W.F. Frieberger, editor-in-chief (Princeton, NJ: Van Nostrand, 1960), p. 135. You should have looked under "Circle of least confusion." And, to add to your confusion, this question is not so much about math as it is about photography. Therefore, the answer may be found in a number of good reference works for the shutterbug. But we digress.

Caught up in a matrix of constants and coefficients? Hung up on the hypotenuse hypothesis? Reeling from rotating ratios and rigid bodies? Consult the *International Dictionary of Applied Mathematics*. As the preface explains, it "defines the terms and describes the methods in the applications of mathematics to thirty-one fields of physical science and engineering." It also includes "four foreign language indices which list alphabetically the French, German, Russian, and Spanish equivalents of the terms defined in this book, accompanied by their English equivalents."

Let us all take comfort in Bertrand Russell's insight: "Mathematics may be defined as the subject in which we never know what we are talking about, nor whether what we are saying is true."

22

Time After Time

It depends on how you count them, but we are going to say "six."

The answer may be found in *Rand McNally Goode's World Atlas*, 17th edition (Chicago, IL: Rand McNally and Company, 1986), p. XVI.

You can also use *Goode's* to locate South Dum-Dum, India, Australia's Disappointment Lake, and Truth or Consequences, New Mexico. It contains maps, tables, and indexes concerning "water resources, minorities, income, education, life expectancy, population change, labor structure, and westward expansion," in addition to its maps of climate, rainfall, and time zones. A special feature is a name pronunciation index. So the next time you visit Chad, you will know how to say "Oum Chalouba" (o͞om-shä-lo͞o'ba—shooby-dooby-do).

23

Don't Play It Again, Sam

The quoted passage is from a John Simon review of Woody Allen's film, "Love and Death." (In this film, Allen attempts to satirize Russian literature and cinema in a relatively sophisticated black comedy.)

The review was reprinted in *Contemporary Literary Criticism* (Detroit: Gale Research Co., 1973-present), vol. 16, p. 7. Titled "Our Movie Comedies Are No Laughing Matter," it first appeared in the *New York Times*, section 2, June 29, 1975, pp. 1 and 15.

"What did Jean-Paul Sartre really think of William Faulkner? Was he as confused by 1,300 word sentences as everyone else? What, if any, is the literary significance of *Absalom, Absalom?* 'What, we ask lamely, was he like?' " (George H. Wolfe)

Contemporary Literary Criticism "presents significant passages from the published criticism of work by well-known creative writers....Each volume...lists about 130 authors, with an average of about five excerpts from critical articles or reviews being given for the work of each author."

Another excellent source you might turn to when researching similar questions is Frank Magill's *Bibliography of Literary Criticism* (Englewood Cliffs, NJ: Salem Press, Inc., 1979).

24

And the Beat Goes On...

The answer is *Howl and Other Poems* by Allen Ginsberg and *On the Road* by Jack Kerouac.

The answer may be found in *The Reader's Encyclopedia of American Literature* by Max J. Herzberg and the staff of the Thomas Y. Crowell Company (New York: Thomas Y. Crowell Co., 1962), p. 67.

England has Shakespeare, France has Voltaire, Russia has Tolstoy, and America, of course, has Stephen King. *The Reader's Encyclopedia of American Literature,* as the preface states, "touches on virtually every subject that is related to American Literature" in its author biographies, bibliographies, and in-depth articles on the schools and movements that have shaped American writing.

Additionally, we recommend the one-volume *Benet's Reader's Encyclopedia,* 3rd edition (New York: Harper & Row, 1987). Like *The Reader's Encyclopedia of American Literature, Benet's* includes biographies, sketches of principal characters, myths, legends, folklore, plot summaries, and accounts of significant schools and movements in literature. However, *Benet's* has the advantage of being "the classic and only encyclopedia of world literature in a single volume."

Learn about the ferocious, warlike Berserker, the frenzy of the Goat Song, and the repartee of the University Wits (a.k.a. the Oxymorons).

25

Kowa Bonga!

The answer is Chief Thunderthud.

The answer may be found in *The Great Television Heroes* by Donald F. Glut and Jim Harmon (New York: Doubleday and Company, Inc., 1975), p. 47.

The Great Television Heroes is "a wonderful, nostalgic trip back to the early days of television — a look at its infancy, with anecdotes galore about the delights and mishaps of that first freewheeling era."

We remember it all so clearly — just as if it were yesterday. Our childlike wonder as those new and mysterious worlds flickered before us: why Lucy had so much " 'splainin' " to do, why Buckwheat was only "otay," and why Ed Sullivan always wore such really big shoes.

According to Duncan Renaldo, "The Cisco Kid," this book records "for your reading pleasure and historical knowledge, the intimate details of television's evolution into the most powerful of all media communications." Hey, Pancho!

PART FOUR

Resources

An Under-$100 At-Home Reference Library

Those of us who do research often — either because we have to, or because we like to — eventually find it necessary to build an At-Home Reference Library. This is a highly subjective collection of books that are usually piled on top of our desks or arranged on a shelf nearby, so we can grab them when the need strikes.

An At-Home Reference Library can make your life easier (by providing you with instant access to facts) and save you time (by eliminating some, but by no means all, trips to an outside library). As the years go by, you'll probably start collecting specialized reference books on topics that interest you. For now, however, we recommend the following VERY BASIC and relatively inexpensive collection of essentials, listed in no particular order.

Whenever possible, we have listed the paperback editions. Please be aware that prices may change without notice; the ones given here are current as of June, 1988. All of these books should be readily available at your local bookstore.

— *Oxford American Dictionary* (New York: Avon Books, 1980), $3.95. A portable pocket dictionary that is "Highly Recommended" by the *Library Journal*, it includes 70,000 entries plus hundreds of footnotes to illustrate proper usage of difficult words.

— *Roget's II: The New Thesaurus* (New York: Berkley Books, 1980), $3.95. All entries are alphabetically listed. Definitions are written dictionary-style.

— William Strunk, Jr. and E.B. White, *The Elements of Style*, Third Edition (New York: MacMillan Publishing Co., Inc., 1979), $3.95. The classic reference for anyone who wants to write well.

— *World Almanac & Book of Facts,* published annually (New York: Scripps-Howard Co., 1988), $5.95.

— *Information Please Almanac,* published annually (Boston: Houghton Mifflin Co., 1988), $5.95.

— Matthew Lesko, *Information U.S.A.,* Revised Edition (New York: Viking Penguin Inc., 1986), $22.95. Provides the names, addresses, and phone numbers of over 10,000 government offices and 3,000 data experts; lists the titles of over 3,000 free or low-cost publications; provides access to $10 billion worth of government statistics and market research, 2 million free or low-cost publications, 700,000 government experts, and much more.

— Dr. Laurence J. Peter, *Peter's Quotations: Ideas For Our Time* (New York: Bantam Books, 1977), $4.95.

— J.M. and M.J. Cohen, editors, *The Penguin Dictionary of Modern Quotations,* Second Edition (New York: Penguin Books, 1980), $6.95.

— *Benet's Reader's Encyclopedia,* Third Edition (New York: Harper & Row, 1987), $35.00. A single-volume encyclopedia of world literature — poets, playwrights, novelists, synopses, historical data, major characters in literature, myths and legends, literary terms, artistic movements, and prize winners. (At the time of this writing, this book was only available in hardback.)

One more we can't resist adding (although it would bring your total to over $100, what's money in the pursuit of knowledge?) is:

— Donald M. Murray, *Write To Learn,* 2nd edition (New York: Holt, Rinehart & Winston, Inc., 1987). This is a textbook, and you would probably have to order it from a bookstore, and it could cost as much as $17.95, but it's worth it (arguably the *best* book available on learning to write).

More Recommended References

WARNING: Reference books can be addicting. The more you have, the more you'll want to have. Following is an abbreviated list of more expensive reference books or collections that we have found irresistible. (Consider this a sort of Wish List for the future.)

— Bernard S. Cayne, editorial director, *Academic American Encyclopedia* (Danbury, CT: Grolier, Inc., 1987), 21 volumes. Although the new *Enclopaedia Britannica* is reputed to be "the most scholarly...in terms of coverage and style," the AAE is the only encyclopedia to enter the Computer Age — as it is available in three electronic formats as well as the printed version. The American Library Association hails the AAE as "the most current and up-to-date encyclopedia in the English language for high school, college, and adult readers." The only drawback to the AAE is its emphasis on breadth rather than depth. However, we recommend the AAE for the contemporary scholarship, the quality of illustrations, the constant process of revision, and the fairness of price.

— C.T. Onions, editor, *Shorter Oxford English Dictionary on Historical Principles*, Third Edition, with addenda (Oxford: Clarendon Press, 1962), 2 volumes. The abridged, and more affordable, edition of the most authoritative dictionary of the English language.

— Bergen and Cornelia Evans, *A Dictionary of Contemporary American Usage* (New York: Random House, 1957). Scholarly, witty, and clear.

— *Oxford Dictionary of Quotations,* Third Edition (New York: Oxford University Press, 1979).

— Mortimer J. Adler and Charles Van Doren, editors, *Great Treasury of Western Thoughts: A Compendium of Important Statements on Man and His Institutions by the Great Thinkers in Western History* (New York: R.R. Bowker Co., 1977).

We also want to point you toward some reference books that are especially *fun to read.* There's been a "publishing explosion" in recent years of fact-filled books written to satisfy our culture's craving for more and more information. Here are some of our personal favorites:

— Lewis H. Lapham, Michael Pollan, and Eric Etheridge, *The Harper's Index Book* (New York: Henry Holt & Co., 1987).

— Judy Jones and William Wilson, *An Incomplete Education* (New York: Ballantine Books, 1987).

— Christopher Cerf and Victor Navasky, *The Experts Speak: The Definitive Compendium of Authoritative Misinformation* (New York: Pantheon Books, 1984).

— Charles Panati, *Extraordinary Origins of Everyday Things* (New York: Harper & Row, 1987).

— Cecil Adams, *The Straight Dope* (New York: Ballantine Books, 1984).

— John Ciardi, *A Browser's Dictionary: A Compendium of Curious Expressions & Intriguing Facts* (New York: Harper & Row, 1980).

— Josefa Heifetz Byrne, *Mrs. Byrne's Dictionary of Unusual, Obscure, and Preposterous Words* (Secaucus, NJ: University Books/Citadel Press, 1974).

— Robert L. Chapman, Ph.D., editor, *American Slang* (New York: Harper & Row, 1987). An abridged edition of *The New Dictionary of American Slang.*

— Fred Metcalf, *The Penguin Dictionary of Modern Humorous Quotations* (New York: Viking Penguin, Inc., 1986).

— Nat Shapiro, *Whatever It Is, I'm Against It* (New York, Simon & Schuster, 1984).

— Don Lessem, *The Worst of Everything* (New York: McGraw-Hill Book Co., 1988).

— William Poundstone, *Big Secrets* (New York: Quill, 1983) and *Bigger Secrets* (Boston: Houghton Mifflin Co., 1986).

— David Feldman, *Why Do Clocks Run Clockwise? and other Imponderables* (New York: Harper & Row, 1987).

— Tom Burnam, *The Dictionary of Misinformation* (New York: Harper & Row, 1975).

— Irving Wallace and David Wallechinsky, *The Book of Lists* (New York: William Morrow & Co., 1977). *Book II* published in 1980.

Finally: In the likely event that you yearn to become even more of an Expert Researcher, we direct you toward the following Recommended References on References — all excellent guides.

— Jacques Barzun and Henry F. Graff, *The Modern Researcher,* Fourth Edition (New York: Harcourt, Brace, Jovanovich, 1985).

— Mona McCormick, *The New York Times Guide to Reference Materials* (New York: New American Library, 1971).

— Bruce L. Felknor, *How To Look Things Up And Find Things Out* (New York: Quill/William Morrow, 1988).

— Robert I. Berkman, *Find It Fast* (New York: Harper & Row, 1987).

References Cited In This Book

STOP!!!

This section is meant as an aid to teachers, librarians, and parents. If you are a student and are reading this BEFORE attempting to find the answers to the questions, then YOU ARE LAZY (not to mention cheating).

Following is a list of the questions, accompanied by the references they are designed to point students toward. You may want to check this list against the references available in the library in which your students will be working.

1. Assessing the SAT
High School: A Report on Secondary Education in America by Ernest Boyer (New York: Harper & Row, 1983, © Carnegie Foundation for the Advancement of Teaching).

2. Ask Not...
The *New York Times*; *The New York Times Index* (New York: New York Times Company; published semimonthly, quarterly, and annually).

3. Nerds and Knotheads
Dictionary of American Slang, Second Supplemented Edition, compiled by Harold Wentworth and Stuart Berg Flexner (New York: Thomas Y. Crowell Company, 1975).

4. Mall-Adjusted
Guinness Book of World Records (New York: Sterling Publishing Co., 1962-date).

5. Back in the U.S.S.R.
Facts on File (New York: Facts on File, 1940 to date); *Facts on File Index.*

6. It Must Be Love
Granger's Index to Poetry, 8th edition, edited by William F. Bernhardt (New York: Columbia University Press, 1986).

7. Bach-Analia
The New Grove Dictionary of Music and Musicians by Sir George Grove (1820-1900), edited by Stanley Sadie (London: MacMillan Publishers Ltd., 1980).

8. Ducks in the Wry
Book Review Digest (New York: Wilson, 1905 to date).

9. A Goldberg Variation
Current Biography Yearbook, volume 46, for 1985 (New York: H.W. Wilson, 1985).

10. Much Ado About Everything
Familiar Quotations by John Bartlett, Fifteenth Edition, edited by Emily Morison Beck (Boston: Little, Brown, and Co., 1980).

11. Rated R
Famous First Facts by Joseph Nathan Kane, 4th edition (New York: H.W. Wilson, 1981).

12. A Conscientious Objection
Congressional Record; Congressional Record Index: Proceedings and Debates of Congress, published biweekly (Washington, D.C.: U.S. Government Printing Office, 1873-present).

13. Oliver Twisted
Statistical Abstracts of the United States (Washington, D.C.: U.S. Department of Commerce, Bureau of the Census; published annually).

14. Gobble Gobble Glup Glup
Morris Dictionary of Word and Phrase Origins (New York: Harper and Row, 1962).

15. Days of Our Lives
The American Book of Days, 3rd edition, by Jane M. Hatch (New York: H.W. Wilson Co., 1978).

16. Moo-Goo-Gai-Panic
Directory of Directories, 5th edition (Detroit: Gale Research Company, 1988).

17. One Small Stumble
The *Reader's Guide to Periodical Literature* (New York: H.W. Wilson Co., 1900-present).

18. You Can Bet on It
Barron's; Business Periodicals Index (New York: H.W. Wilson, 1958 to date).

19. Gogh for It
Encyclopedia of World Art, edited by Bernard S. Meyers (New York: McGraw-Hill, 1959).

20. Tank U.
Official 1987-1988 Congressional Directory (Washington, D.C.: U.S. Government Printing Office, 1809-date).

21. Math According to Miss Margarida
International Dictionary of Applied Mathematics, W.F. Frieberger, editor-in-chief (Princeton, NJ: Van Nostrand, 1960), p. 135.

22. Time After Time
Rand McNally Goode's World Atlas, 17th edition (Chicago, IL: Rand McNally and Company, 1986).

23. Don't Play It Again, Sam
Contemporary Literary Criticism (Detroit: Gale Research Co., 1973-present).

24. And the Beat Goes On...
The Reader's Encyclopedia of American Literature by Max J. Herzberg and the staff of the Thomas Y. Crowell Company (New York: Thomas Y. Crowell Co., 1962).

25. Kowa Bonga!
The Great Television Heroes by Donald F. Glut and Jim Harmon (New York: Doubleday and Company, Inc., 1975).

About the Author

Nationally recognized and honored for innovation in curriculum development, Randall McCutcheon was selected as Nebraska's Teacher of the Year in 1985. More recently, in 1987, he was honored as the National Forensic League's National "Coach of the Year."

From 1975-1985 he was Director of Forensics at Lincoln East High School in Nebraska, and from 1985-1988 he was Co-Director of Forensics at Milton Academy in Massachusetts. Currently he teaches English and is Director of Forensics at Albuquerque Academy in Albuquerque, New Mexico.

He is also the author of *Get Off My Brain: A Survival Guide for Lazy Students,* published by Free Spirit Publishing.

Other Books By Free Spirit Publishing

GET OFF MY BRAIN
A Survival Guide For Lazy Students
by Randall McCutcheon

DIRECTORY OF AMERICAN YOUTH ORGANIZATIONS
A Guide To Over 400 Clubs, Groups, Troops, Teams, Societies,
Lodges, and More for Young People
by Judith B. Erickson

FIGHTING INVISIBLE TIGERS
A Stress Management Guide For Teens
by Earl Hipp

PERFECTIONISM
What's Bad About Being Too Good
by Miriam Adderholdt-Elliott

THE GIFTED KIDS SURVIVAL GUIDES
by Judy Galbraith

Write or call for a free copy of our catalog:

Free Spirit Publishing
123 N. Third St., Suite 716
Minneapolis, MN 55401

(612) 338-2068

028.7076 M139c 1989

McCutcheon, Randall, 1949—

Can you find it?

028.7076 M139c 1989

McCutcheon, Randall, 1949—

Can you find it?